Principles of Evidence in Public International Law as Applied by Investor-State Tribunals

International Investment Law and Arbitration

Volumes published in this Brill Research Perspectives title are listed at *brill.com/rpia*

Principles of Evidence in Public International Law as Applied by Investor-State Tribunals

Burden and Standards of Proof

By

Kabir Duggal and Wendy W. Cai

BRILL

LEIDEN | BOSTON

This paperback book edition is simultaneously published as Volume 2(2) 2018, in *International Investment Law and Arbitration*, DOI:10.1163/24055778-12340005.

Library of Congress Control Number: 2018964458

Typeface for the Latin, Greek, and Cyrillic scripts: "Brill". See and download: brill.com/brill-typeface.

ISBN 978-90-04-36642-8 (paperback)
ISBN 978-90-04-39061-4 (e-book)

This book is printed on acid-free paper and produced in a sustainable manner.

Contents

Principles of Evidence in Public International Law as Applied by Investor-State Tribunals: Burden and Standards of Proof

*Kabir Duggal**
Senior Associate, Arnold & Porter; Lecturer-in-Law, Columbia Law School
kduggal@law.columbia.edu

Wendy W. Cai
Associate, Gibson, Dunn & Crutcher
wendy.cai@columbia.edu

Abstract

Principles of Evidence in Public International Law as Applied by Investor-State Tribunals explores the fundamental principles of evidence and how these principles relating to burden of proof and standards of proof are derived.

By tracing the applications of major principles recognized by the International Court of Justice and applied by investor-state tribunal jurisprudence, the authors offer valuable insight into the interpretation, understanding, and nuances of indispensable principles of evidence, an area that has been ignored in both investor-state arbitration and public international law more generally. Each principle is analyzed through historical and modern lenses to provide clarity and cohesion in understanding how fundamental principles of evidence will affect evidentiary dispositions of parties in investment arbitration and public international law cases.

Keywords

investment arbitration – evidence – evidentiary principles – burden of proof – standard of proof – public international law

•••

* The views in this article are solely the authors' and not of their respective firms. The authors reserve the rights to update or change the positions stated herein based, *inter alia*, on how the jurisprudence develops.

 | DOI:10.1163/9789004390614_002

> Uh ... everything that guy just said is bullshit.... Thank you.
>
> VINNY GAMBINI in the movie "My Cousin Vinny" before the Judge

⁂

I Introduction

In any trial or arbitration, principles of evidence are fundamental in ensuring a fair hearing.[1] In the international arbitration world, arbitrators are given the power to decide evidentiary issues, including decisions regarding admissibility, relevance, and probative value of the evidence proffered.[2] When parties establish arbitration tribunals, rarely are explicit or implicit rules of procedure and evidence found in these agreements to arbitrate.[3] Arbitral tribunals enjoy vast amounts of freedom in establishing, implementing, and applying evidentiary rules.

Evidentiary matters in investor-state arbitration are particularly significant with the presence of a state as one of the parties to a case because this implicates principles of international law in the debate. The majority of evidentiary rules in investor-state arbitration, however, are inspired from general principles of law that have been established since the early 20th century through international tribunals like the Permanent Court of International Justice (PCIJ) and the International Court of Justice (ICJ).

Two of the most important standards in evidentiary matters concern burden of proof and standards of proof. While there are certainly many more issues surrounding the principles of evidence, as shown in Table 1, including issues regarding document production, witness evidence, and expert evidence, these two are unavoidable issues in any legal proceeding. What is particularly significant here is that most arbitral rules do not provide any detailed guidance on burden and standards of proof, in contrast to most domestic legal proceedings.[4]

1 CHITTHARANJAN AMERASINGHE, EVIDENCE IN INTERNATIONAL LITIGATION 66 (2005).

2 *See, e.g.*, ICSID Convention, Art. 43; ICSID Arbitration Rules 34; ICSID Additional Facility Rules, Art. 41; 1976 UNCITRAL Arbitration Rules, Art. 24; 2013 UNCITRAL Arbitration Rules, Art. 27; 1998 ICC Rules of Arbitration, Arts. 20, 22; 2017 ICC Rules of Arbitration, Arts. 25, 27; 2014 LCIA Arbitration Rules, Arts. 15, 22; 2017 Stockholm Chamber of Commerce Arbitration Rules, Arts. 29, 31.

3 AMERASINGHE, *supra* note 1 at 47.

4 *See generally* Michelle Terezinha Grando, The Process of Fact-Finding Before International Tribunals: A Study of the WTO Dispute Settlement System, Graduate Department

TABLE 1 Evidentiary principles under major arbitral rules

Arbitral rules	Tribunal's ability to order production of evidence	Tribunal's free assessment of evidence	Burden of proof	Standard of proof
International Centre for Settlement of Investment Disputes ("ICSID") Convention[5]	Yes (Convention, Art. 43; Rules 34, 54)	Yes (Rule 34)	Not addressed	Not addressed
2013 United Nations Commission on International Trade Law ("UNCITRAL") Arbitration Rules[6]	Yes (Art. 27)	Yes (Art. 27)	Yes (Art. 27)[7]	Not addressed
2017 International Chamber of Commerce ("ICC") Rules of Arbitration[8]	Yes (Art. 25)	Not addressed	Not addressed	Not addressed
2017 Stockholm Chamber of Commerce ("SCC") Rules of Arbitration[9]	Yes (Art. 31(2))	Yes (Art. 31(1))	Not addressed	Not addressed

of Law—University of Toronto 85 (2008) ("The question of the standard of proof has been similarly neglected in proceedings before international courts and tribunals. The statutes and rules of international courts and tribunals such as the ICJ and the Iran-United States Tribunal are silent on the issue. Nor has the jurisprudence of those bodies elaborated on the standard of proof that must be satisfied to prove a proposition.").

5 ICSID Convention, Regulations, and Rules (2006), *available at* https://icsid.worldbank.org/en/documents/icsiddocs/icsid%20convention%20english.pdf.

6 UNCITRAL Arbitration Rules (as revised in 2010), *available at* https://www.uncitral.org/pdf/english/texts/arbitration/arb-rules-revised/arb-rules-revised-2010-e.pdf.

7 UNCITRAL Rules, Article 27(1) (2013) ("Each party shall have the burden of proving the facts relied on to support its claim or defence."). *See also* Peter Binder, Analytical Commentary to the UNCITRAL Arbitration Rules 262 (2013) (discussing negotiating history where drafters rejected the inclusion of the phrase "save as otherwise provided by the applicable law ..." before the text of Article 27(1) because the draft of Article 27(1) did not prevent the application of regulations on the burden of proof in the applicable law.); Sophie Nappert, Commentary on the UNCITRAL Arbitration Rules 2010: A Practitioner's Guide 103–04 (2012) ("This statement of principle [regarding Article 27(1)] had proven useful, notably in investor-to-State arbitration. It was also found in a number of institutional arbitration rules.").

8 ICC, Arbitration Rules (2017), *available at* https://cdn.iccwbo.org/content/uploads/sites/3/2017/01/ICC-2017-Arbitration-and-2014-Mediation-Rules-english-version.pdf.pdf.

9 SCC, Arbitration Rules (2017), *available at* https://sccinstitute.com/media/169838/arbitration_rules_eng_17_web.pdf.

This is not unique to investor-state arbitration. The rules for several international institutions do not provide any detailed guidance on evidentiary issues as demonstrated in Table 2 below.

TABLE 2 Evidentiary principles under international institutions

CATEGORY	Institution's ability to order production of evidence	Institution's free assessment of evidence	Burden of proof	Standard of proof
PCIJ[10]	Yes (Art. 48, 52)	Implicit in judicial function	Not addressed	Not addressed
ICJ[11]	Yes (Art. 62, 66)	Implicit in judicial function	Not addressed	Not addressed
World Trade Organization ("WTO")[12]	Yes (Art. 13)	Implicit in judicial function	Not addressed[13]	Not addressed[14]
Maritime Arbitration Association of the US[15]	Yes (Art. 20)	Yes (Art. 20)	Yes (Art. 20)	Yes (Art. 28)

10 Statute of the Permanent Court of International Justice (PCIJ), 16 December 1920 (Amended by the Protocol of September 14, 1929), *available at* http://www.icj-cij.org/files/permanent-court-of-international-justice/serie_D/D_01_4e_edition.pdf.

11 Statute of the International Court of Justice (ICJ), 14 April 1978 (Amended on April 14, 2005).

12 World Trade Organization (WTO), Dispute Settlement Understanding (DSU) Annex 2, Understanding on Rules and Procedures Governing the Settlement Of Disputes, *available at* https://www.wto.org/english/Tratop_e/dispu_e/dsu_e.htm.

13 *See* James H. Pfitzer & Sheila Sabune, Burden of Proof in WTO Dispute Settlement: Contemplating Preponderance of the Evidence, 9 ICSID DISPUTE SETTLEMENT AND LEGAL ASPECTS OF INT'L TRADE 6 (April 2009) (explaining that WTO DSU "incorporated at least two rules relevant to the burden of proof ...[f]irst, the complaining party is required to prove all violations alleged by it. Second, a respondent who invokes general exceptions ... is obliged to prove that the necessary requirements for the exceptions are satisfied."). *See also* Legal issues arising in WTO dispute settlement proceedings, WTO website, *available at* https://www.wto.org/english/tratop_e/dispu_e/disp_settlement_cbt_e/c10s6p1_e.htm ("The DSU does not include any express rule concerning the burden of proof in panel proceedings.").

14 James H. Pfitzer & Sheila Sabun, *supra* note 13 at 7–8 (discussing prima facie standard used in WTO arbitration proceedings).

15 Maritime Arbitration Association of the United States, Arbitration Rules, *available at* http://www.maritimearbitration.com/File-a-Case/Arbitration-Rules.

Because of the significance of the burden of and standard of proof for any party in a legal proceeding, this article will focus on these two topics. ICJ jurisprudence has recognized numerous burden of proof principles that are generally followed by investor-state tribunals. These principles are explored in Part II of this article. Standard of proof principles are more ambiguous, with a wider dispersion in how tribunals implement these principles to hearings. Relevant case law from the ICJ and investor-state tribunals illustrate that a relative approach is taken by weighing a multitude of considerations that are explained in Part III. Part IV provides a conclusion.

1 *Burden of Proof and Standard of Proof*

1.1 Burden of Proof

A fundamental issue in any legal proceeding is which party must prove a particular issue. Burden of proof is defined as "the duty of a party to persuade the trier of fact by the end of the case of the truth of certain propositions."[16] In other words, burden of proof answers the question "who" has to prove or convince a tribunal of a fact. This principle has historical origins across the world, in both civil and common law jurisdictions.[17] Numerous international dispute resolution bodies, including the PCIJ, ICJ, and WTO dispute settlement panels have recognized this principle as well.[18] Investor-state

16 J.D. HEYDON, CASES AND MATERIALS ON EVIDENCE 13 (Butterworths, London, 1975).

17 BIN CHENG, GENERAL PRINCIPLES OF LAW AS APPLIED BY INTERNATIONAL COURTS AND TRIBUNALS 327 (2006) ("With regard to the incidence of the burden of proof in particular, international judicial decisions are not wanting which expressly hold that there exists a general principle of law placing the burden of proof upon the claimant and that this principle is applicable to international judicial proceedings. In *The Queen Case* (1872), for instance, it was held that:—'One must follow, as a general rule of solution, the principle of jurisprudence accepted by the law of all countries, that it is for the claimant to make the proof of his claim'."). See also V.S. Mani, INTERNATIONAL ADJUDICATION: PROCEDURAL ASPECTS (Martinus Nijhoff Publishers 1980) 202; Mojtaba Kazazi, BURDEN OF PROOF AND RELATED ISSUES: A STUDY ON EVIDENCE BEFORE INTERNATIONAL TRIBUNALS (Kluwer Law International 1996) 51; Chittharanjan F. Amerasinghe, EVIDENCE IN INTERNATIONAL LITIGATION (Martinus Nijhoff Publishers 2005) 61–62; ANNA RIDDELL & BRENDAN PLANT, EVIDENCE BEFORE THE INTERNATIONAL COURT OF JUSTICE 87 (2009); Jeffrey Waincymer, PROCEDURE AND EVIDENCE IN INTERNATIONAL ARBITRATION (Wolters Kluwer 2012) 762–64.

18 See DURWARD V SANDIFER, EVIDENCE BEFORE INTERNATIONAL TRIBUNALS 126–127 (1939) ("This burden may rest on the defendant, if there be a defendant, equally with the plaintiff, as the former may incur the burden of substantiating any proposition he asserts in answer to the allegations of the plaintiff."); Anna Riddell, 'Evidence, Fact-Finding, and Experts' in Cesare P.R. Romano, Karen J. Alter & Yuval Shany (eds), THE OXFORD HANDBOOK OF INTERNATIONAL ADJUDICATION 858–59 (2014) ("[C]ourts of law have relied on the maxim actori incumbit onus probandi or "the claimant carries the burden of proof.... various international adjudicative bodies, including several arbitral tribunals,

tribunals have clarified that burden of proof is an absolute issue of determining "which party has to prove what, in order for its case to prevail."[19] The party which has the burden of proof bears "the risk of non-persuasion of the Tribunal."[20]

The party setting forth a proposition (whether the claimant or respondent) carries the burden of proof because the tribunal cannot establish the veracity of any facts set forth by a party nor can it render a *non-liquet* judgment.[21] This is true in public international law in general, as the courts themselves are not the ones who are responsible for ascertaining facts, so the burden falls mainly to the parties themselves.[22]

To commentators like V.S. Mani, burden of proof "represents a specific crystallization of the general obligation of the parties to present evidence."[23] This suggests that discharging burden of proof requires a party to present evidence.[24] While some national legal systems derive a slightly different meaning from "burden of proof" than the meaning it holds in international law, those differences are slight.[25]

---

the PCIJ, the ICJ, and human rights bodies have consistently applied the actori incumbit probatio rule."); WTO, United States—Measure Affecting Imports of Woven Wool Shirts and Blouses from India (April 25, 1997) WT/DS33/AB/R [14]; Joost Pauwelyn, *Evidence, Proof and Persuasion in WTO Dispute Settlement: Who Bears the Burden?*, 1 J. of Int'l Econ. L. 227, 237–38 (2006) ("The first rule: it is for the complaining party to prove GATT violations it alleges … The second rule: it is for the party invoking an exception or defence to prove it."); Michelle T. Grando, *Allocating The Burden of Proof in WTO Disputes: A Critical Analysis*, 9 J. of Int'l Econ. L. 615, 618 ("[I]t would seem that the question of the allocation of the burden of proof would have been settled: the complainant would have to prove the violations of the agreements that he alleged, and the defendant would have the burden of proving any exceptions contained in those agreements." The author then describes how the application of this maxim in the WTO context poses serious problems in identifying the "general rule" and the "exception" but does not call into question the validity of the maxim itself.).

19 *The Rompetrol Group N.V. v Romania*, ICSID Case No ARB/06/3, at 178 (2013).

20 *Noble Ventures, Inc v Romania*, ICSID Case No ARB/01/11, Award 100 (October 12, 2005).

21 AMERASINGHE, *supra* note 1 at 36. *See also Windstream Energy LLC v Government of Canada*, PCA Case No 2013–22, Award 351 (September 27, 2016) ("the Tribunal cannot simply declare *non liquet*."). *Non liquet* refers to a situation where a tribunal refuses to make a finding because the matter is not clear.

22 CHENG, *supra* note 17 at 302 (2006).

23 V.S. MANI, *supra* note 17 (1980).

24 MOJTABA KAZAZI, *supra* note 17, 40 (Kluwer Law International 1995).

25 In civil law countries, the burden of proof is limited to the duty of a party in proving the allegations that it makes. In contrast, in common law countries, the burden of proof often includes both the persuasive burden as well as the legal burden of producing sufficient

1.2 Standard of Proof

The standard of proof stems from the duty of tribunals to decide whether or not a party putting forth a claim has succeeded in proving this particular claim.[26] It "relates to the quantum or degree of proof, i.e. by what measure is what the claimant has to prove to be judged."[27] Standard of proof answers the question "how much?". Leading commentators in the public international law sphere use standard of proof to determine the character and sufficiency of evidence needed to establish a particular fact in question.[28]

Scholars have developed a definition for standard of proof:

> The standard of proof is the measure against which 'the value of each piece of evidence as well as the overall value of the evidence in a given case should be weighed and determined', and justice generally requires that all evidence be treated equally and subjected to the same measure. It is noteworthy that the Court must not only evaluate whether each particular fact has been established, but must also assess whether the case as a whole has been made out on the basis of these proven facts, as well as any facts agreed by the parties, or judicially noted.[29]

Investor-state tribunals have explained that standard of proof is a relative question of "how much evidence is needed to establish either an individual issue or the party's case as a whole".[30] There is great flexibility, however, in how tribunals address standard of proof with parties during arbitration proceedings. Investor-state tribunals sometimes do not discuss the standard of

---

evidence. Common law jurisdictions also sometimes divide adjudication of fact versus law between a jury and a judge, which results in a burden of proof that must be proven in a two-step process. Civil law jurisdictions do not face this division, since judges adjudicate both law and fact. There are, of course, scholarly disagreements and criticisms that stem from the exact differences between burden of proof in civil versus common law jurisdictions. *See* KAZAZI, *supra* note 24 at 23 (discussing differences between the civil law and common law systems); SIR RUPERT CROSS, CROSS ON EVIDENCE 87 (5th ed. 1979).

26 AMERASINGHE, *supra* note 1 at 232.

27 AMERASINGHE, *supra* note 1 at 232.

28 NATHAN D. O'MALLEY, RULES OF EVIDENCE IN INTERNATIONAL ARBITRATION: AN ANNOTATED GUIDE 207 (Informa 2012) ("The standard of proof is used to determine whether the evidence a party has produced in support of its factual allegations is sufficient to establish the facts in question.").

29 RIDDELL & PLANT, *supra* note 17, at 123 (citing partially KAZAZI, *supra* note 17, at 323).

30 *The Rompetrol Group N.V. v Romania*, ICSID Case No ARB/06/3 178 (2013).

proof that is imposed at all,[31] but at other times provide general evidentiary parameters.[32]

Common and civil law systems differ greatly when it comes to the standard of proof they utilize.[33] The chief difference is that common law divides burden of proof into both a procedural and substantive issue, whereas civil law focuses only on the substantive.[34] In common law systems, judges generally apply preponderance of evidence as the standard of proof in civil cases.[35] Preponderance of the evidence translates to more-likely-than-not, though there is debate as to the practical meaning of this standard. This is especially true considering the number of variables in rendering a verdict: lay jurors, effect of voting in a group, and psychological relativity when it comes to more-likely-than-not.[36] Criminal standards in common law systems like the United States often differ and require proof beyond a reasonable doubt.

In civil law countries, the "inner conviction" test, where an arbitrator must be personally convinced of the evidence produced, seems to be the most important factor.[37] A party must convince the judge that their assertions are true.[38] In explaining this principle, German treatises have clarified that "[t]he judge may and must always content himself with a degree of certainty that is appropriate for practical life, one which silences doubts without entirely excluding them."[39] This is comparable to a reasonable doubt standard, and this standard holds true in German law regardless of whether the lawsuit is a private

---

31 *Schering Corporation Case* 375 (1984) (Mosk, dissenting) ("It is regrettable that the Tribunal has never discussed the standard of proof it imposes on parties."); *see also* KAZAZI, *supra* note 17, at 323–324 ("The scope of the standard of proof, considered broadly, may be formulated in the question, 'how should the burden of proof be discharged?' This question covers a wide range of issues related to the details of production, admissibility and evaluation of evidence, such as time, order, language, and type of evidence to be produced.").

32 *See, e.g.*, *Flexi-Van Leasing, Inc. case*, Order of 20 December 1982, 1 *Iran-US CTR*, p. 455–63; *General Motors Corporation Case*, Order of 21 January 1983, 3 *Iran-US CTR*, pp. 1–2.

33 Kevin M. Clermont & Emily Sherwin, *A Comparative View of Standards of Proof*, 50 AM. J. COMP. L. 243, 254 (2002).

34 RIDDELL & PLANT, *supra* note 17, at 81.

35 AMERASINGHE, *supra* note 1, at 233.

36 Kevin M. Clermont, *Procedure's Magical Number Three: Psychological Bases for Standards of Decision*, 72 CORNELL L. REV. 1115, at 1119 n. 13, 1147–48 (1987).

37 AMERASINGHE, *supra* note 1, at 233; Jochen A. Frowein, *Fact-Finding by the European Commission on Human Rights*, in FACT-FINDING BY INTERNATIONAL TRIBUNALS 248 (Lillich ed. 1991).

38 Clermont & Sherwin, *supra* note 33, at 243.

39 Benjamin Kaplan, Arthur T. von Mehren & Rudolf Schaefer, *Phases of German Civil Procedure I*, 71 HARV. L. REV. 1193 (1957) (quoting 1 STEIN & JONAS § 286, comm. I(1)). *See also B. v Kind B.*, 7 B.G.H.Z. 116 (4th Civ. Sen., July 14, 1952).

(including civil), criminal, or public law matter, with some limited exceptions.[40] Other civil countries, especially those in Europe, follow this standard as well.[41]

Despite the difference in terminology between civil and common law standards, for all practical purposes in any investor-state arbitration, the application of both will be the same.[42] It is important to harmonize an understanding for standard of proof in arbitral tribunals, since practitioners from states around the world in investor-state arbitrations come into the arbitration with different backgrounds and experiences regarding standard of proof. Without a standardized law for investor-state arbitration, states and attorneys representing investors will likely draw on their own domestic training, which leads to incongruity in expectations.

In international arbitration, the governing law may be the one that requires a certain standard. That standard may be one that is required by the chosen law, or one that is chosen by agreement of the parties themselves.[43] Possible

---

40 JULIANE KOKOTT, THE BURDEN OF PROOF IN COMPARATIVE AND INTERNATIONAL HUMAN RIGHTS LAW 18 (1996); Clermont & Sherwin, *supra* note 33, at 245.

41 MARY ANN GLENDON, MICHAEL WALLACE GORDON & CHRISTOPHER OSAKWE, COMPARATIVE LEGAL TRADITIONS 903 (1985) (explaining that Soviet law required only "inner conviction of the judge" in both civil and criminal cases).

42 Many commentators use civil and common law terminologies interchangeably. *See, e.g.*, Julian D.M. Lew, 'Document Disclosure, Evidentiary Value of Documents and Burden of Evidence' in Teresa Giovannini & Alexis Mouree (eds), *Written Evidence and Discovery in International Arbitration: New Issues and Tendencies* 22 (Dossiers ICC Institute of World Business Law 2009) ("In practice, the standard of proof in arbitration requires a level that persuades the tribunal in one's favour. This will inevitably be a balance of probabilities. In practice, this will be whether the tribunal is satisfied, or believes, on the basis of the evidence, that the claims or defences are substantiated."); A.T. Martin, *International Arbitration and Corruption: An Evolving Standard* (2004) Transnational Dispute Management 7, *available at* https://www.transnational-dispute-management.com/article.asp?key=88 ("The standard of proof for civil litigation in England is the 'balance of probabilities.' In civil law jurisdictions, the judge seeks an 'inner conviction' in determining the facts. These various standards are viewed as having little difference."); George M. von Mehren & Claudia T. Salomon, *Submitting Evidence in International Arbitration: The Common Lawyer's Guide* (2003) Journal of International Arbitration 285, 291 ("A general, underlying standard, an elevated burden of proof, and a very low standard or insufficient explanation of the reasoning. Regarding the first, a general standard is one that is better explained to common law lawyers as a balance of probabilities, i.e., the evidence must be something more likely true than not true but not so high as required for criminal convictions. Civil lawyers, in contrast, are more accustomed to what may be a higher burden of proof referring to the inner conviction of the judge. In any event, the strategic mind of the counsel must remember that in all cases, the real general standard is and must be a test of preponderance of evidence.").

43 AMERASINGHE, *supra* note 1 at 234. *See also* Reymond, *The Practical Distinction Between the Burden of Proof and Taking of Evidence—A Further Perspective*, 10 ARBITRATION INT'L

standards include preponderance of evidence, proof in a convincing manner, and proof beyond a reasonable doubt.[44]

The preponderance of evidence standard is based on whether evidence is more likely than not; it is otherwise known as the balance of probabilities standard or the reasonable degree of probability standard. Preponderance of evidence is the most commonly used standard in both the ICJ and investor-state tribunals.[45] The proof in a convincing manner standard is a heightened standard that some tribunals take in cases where serious claims are made against States. Several examples appear in Part III.

Proof beyond a reasonable doubt, on the other hand, is a standard usually reserved for criminal hearings that would not apply to most civil arbitration proceedings.[46] However, a few instances in the jurisprudence highlight when this standard may be used. These standards have been developed through international tribunals' rules, hearings, and decisions.

2 *History of PCIJ/ICJ as Related to Evidence*

The PCIJ, a precursor to the ICJ, was established by the League of Nations as the first permanently constituted international tribunal with general jurisdiction.[47] Its purpose was to resolve disputes that arose in international law, and from 1922 to 1940, it recognized many principles in international law, including basic principles relating to evidentiary matters. In the PCIJ Rules itself, there are broad and unspecific provisions for procuring and admitting evidence.[48] One of the most relevant rules, Article 48, states that:

> The Court may, subject to the provision of Article 44 of the Statute, invite the parties to call witnesses, or may call for the production of any other evidence on points of fact in regard to which the parties are not in agreement.[49]

---

326 (1994); Frowein, *supra* note 37, at 246; Thomas Buergenthal, *Judicial Fact-Finding: The Inter-American Human Rights Court*, in FACT-FINDING BY INTERNATIONAL TRIBUNALS 271 (Lillich ed. 1991), CHITTHARANJAN AMERASINGHE, LAW OF THE INTERNATIONAL CIVIL SERVICE 612 (1994).

44 AMERASINGHE, *supra* note 1 at 233–235.

45 FROWEIN, *supra* note 13, 9 at 23 (2009).

46 AMERASINGHE, *supra* note 1 at 233–235.

47 Permanent Court of International Justice, *available at* http://www.icj-cij.org/en/pcij.

48 PCIJ, Revised Rules of Court (July 31, 1926).

49 *Id.* at 54.

This provision appears to be similar to previous rules taken from the 1899 and 1907 Hague Conventions for the Pacific Settlement of International Disputes.[50] When this article was proposed to be incorporated into the PCIJ, the Drafting Committee intended to give preference to a system where any evidence produced by the parties was to be admitted.[51] The rules remained silent on the burden and standard of proof. Thus, it was up to the PCIJ tribunals to develop and provide guidance on the standards for the burden and standard of proof.

In 1923, the PCIJ made a general observation on evidentiary burdens in the *Eastern Carelia* case. The court noted that "the facts upon which the opinion of the Court is desired should not be controversy, and it should not be left to the Court itself to ascertain what they are."[52] This is probably because especially in contentious proceedings, parties hold the burden of presenting evidence.[53] The general approach the PCIJ took was to first establish undisputed facts and rely on those, and then identify the disputed issues for consideration.[54]

The PCIJ stopped hearing cases and was dissolved during World War II, but the need for an international tribunal prompted the creation of the ICJ in 1945.[55] Just two years after its creation, the ICJ heard its first case—the *Corfu Channel* case, which immediately advanced the development of evidentiary principles. In the decision, the court describes *prima facie* responsibility and the principle of shifting the burden of evidence.[56] The Court also describes

50 *See, e.g.*, Hague Convention for the Pacific Settlement of Disputes, Arts. 43, 44, 47 (1899) ("Article 43 The Tribunal is free to take into consideration fresh Acts or documents to which its attention may be drawn by the agents or counsel of the parties. In this case, the Tribunal has the right to require the production of these Acts or documents, but is obliged to make them known to the opposite party ... Article 47 The members of the Tribunal have the right to put questions to the agents and counsel of the parties, and to demand explanations from them on doubtful points."); Hague Convention for the Pacific Settlement of Disputes, Art. 68, 69, 72 (1907) ("Article 69 The Tribunal can, besides, require from the agents of the parties the production of all papers, and can demand all necessary explanations. In case of refusal the Tribunal takes note of it ..."); Eduardo Valencia-Ospina, Evidence Before the International Court of Justice, 1 INT'L L. FORUM DU DROIT INT'L 202, 202 (1999).

51 PCIJ, Twenty-Fifth Meeting, Continuation of the discussion on the Draft Rules of Court submitted by the Drafting Committee 142 (March 9, 1922), *available at* https://www.icj-cij.org/files/permanent-court-of-international-justice/serie_D/D_02_preparation_reglement.pdf.

52 *Status of Eastern Carelia*, PCIJ, Series B, No. 5, at 28.

53 Andreas Zimmermann, et al., The Statute of the International Court of Justice: A Commentary 1680 (2d ed. 2012).

54 KAZAZI, *supra* note 17 at 75.

55 History, *available at* http://www.icj-cij.org/en/history.

56 *Id.*

methods of evidence and their weight in making a judgment. Mere conjectures, for instance, would not be considered proof at all.[57] Indirect evidence, such as inferences of fact and circumstantial evidence, is permitted and considered.[58] However, while such inferential evidence is permissible, the Court requires "*no room* for reasonable doubt" in its examination.[59]

The ICJ Rules of Court also address certain evidentiary issues. Article 62 of the Rules of Court in the ICJ embraces the wide breadth of the powers of the Court when it comes to the taking of evidence:

> [t]he Court may at any time call upon the parties to produce such evidence or to give such explanations the Court may consider to be necessary for the elucidation of any aspect of the matters in issue, or may itself seek other information for this purpose.[60]

Similar to the PCIJ, while the ICJ Rules of Court give the court wide discretion on evidence, it lacks specificity when it comes to the principles regarding burden and standard of proof.

Despite the lack of formal guidance in its Rules, the ICJ has developed more specific evidentiary burden principles through case law. For example, the *Nicaragua Case* (Merits) addressed the issue of proof of facts where the respondent party did not appear before the court.[61] This issue is encapsulated in Article 53(2) of the Statute of the ICJ, which addresses the instance when one party does not appear.[62] According to Rule 53(2), the court is required to

---

57 *Corfu Channel Case (Merits) (U.K. v Albania)*, Judgment of April 9, 1949, 1949 ICJ Rep. 4, 17 (an assertion by Albanian counsel that a minefield might have been laid by the Greek government with no basis of evidence was considered conjecture that was ignored and not considered proof); *see also id.* at 38 ("[T]he Court is confronted with suspicions, conjectures and presumptions, the foundations for which ... are too uncertain to justify [the Judges] in imputing to a State the responsibility for a grave delinquency in international law.").

58 *Id.* at 18 ("[T]he victim of a breach of international law is often unable to furnish direct proof of facts giving rise to responsibility. Such a State should be allowed a more liberal recourse to inferences of fact and circumstantial evidence. This indirect evidence is admitted in all systems of law, and its use is recognized by international decisions. It must be regarded as of special weight when it is based on a series of facts linked together and leading logically to a single conclusion.").

59 *Id.*

60 ICJ, Article 62, The Rules of Court, *available at* http://www.icj-cij.org/documents/index.php?p1=4&p2=3&p3=0.

61 AMERASINGHE, *supra* note 1 at 240.

62 ICJ, Article 53, The Rules of Court ("1. Whenever one of the parties does not appear before the Court, or fails to defend its case, the other party may call upon the Court to decide in favor of its claim. 2. The Court must, before doing so, satisfy itself, not only that it has

"satisfy itself … that the claim is well founded in fact and law."[63] While this does not directly state a standard of proof in regards to facts, the court explains in *Nicaragua* that the term "satisfy itself" implies that the Court "must attain the same degree of certainty as in any other case …, so far as the nature of the case permits, that the facts on which [the claim] is based are supported by convincing evidence."[64] The Court, therefore, clarifies that even if a party refuses to participate in a legal proceeding, there would be no adverse finding or default judgment on this ground alone. In other words, evidentiary standards are not relaxed because of non-participation by a party.

The ICJ interpretation of standard of proof, however, is not as clearly set forth.[65] Commentators such as Amerasinghe have noted the uncertainty involving standard of proof at the ICJ:

> It would seem that both the ICJ and other international tribunals, including arbitral tribunals, which have adjudicated numerous international claims have usually not discussed in detail the matter of the standard of proof to be applied to the evaluated evidence and have not clearly explained the underlying standard they have applied in their decisions. On account of this a judge of the Iran-US Claims Tribunal was prompted to remark: "It is regrettable that the Tribunal has never discussed the standard of proof it imposes on parties." In some cases, however, international tribunals have addressed this question, in order to provide a general guideline for the evidentiary requirements in the cases being decided by them. It may appear that the answer to the question, what is an acceptable standard of proof for international tribunals, depends to some extent on the fact that in this regard there is subjectivity in judgment.[66]

jurisdiction in accordance with Articles 36 and 37, but also that the claim is well founded in fact and law.").

63 1986 ICJ Reports at 24.

64 1986 ICJ Reports at 24; AMERASINGHE, *supra* note 1 at 240–241.

65 RIDDELL & PLANT, *supra* note 17, at 123 ("If the matter of the burden of proof seems complicated in the context of the ICJ, the standard of proof is even more so. The difficulties have their root once again, in the contrasts of the common and civil legal traditions. Whilst there is general agreement in both traditions as to the ultimate rule on the burden of proof, and merely an additional stage or element to the common law burden, with regard to the standard of proof the difference is far more pronounced, and this is apparent throughout the jurisprudence of the Court. Naturally, the matter is of much importance to States who litigate before the Court, and certainty, or at least some general indication as to the appropriate standard, would be desirable. It appears however that the Court prefers not to provide a definitive standard, most probably because the Judges from the different legal traditions cannot agree.").

66 AMERSINGHE, *supra* note 1, at 232–233.

Where evidence is too difficult to obtain or unavailable, the burden of proof should not be "so stringent as to render the proof unduly exacting."[67] For parties that come forth to the ICJ to resolve their disputes, differences in civil and common law backgrounds regarding standard of proof only add to potential conflicts of understanding. The ICJ does not formally delineate standard of proof in their rules, and this is likely due to the differing backgrounds of the ICJ judges as well.[68]

As cases brought forth in the ICJ and in investor-state arbitrations involve ever-increasingly complex issues of both fact and law, an understanding of the modern landscape of evidentiary principles is crucial. The next parts of this article seek to explore the evidentiary principles that have evolved from the PCIJ/ICJ jurisprudence, and also to investigate the effect these principles have had on investor-state arbitration. The principles set forth are those that apply generally to evidentiary matters, as seen through the convergence of jurisprudence on these principles. Although some nuances are noted, this article does not purport nor intend to cover all the possible evidentiary difficulties that tribunals have and must deal with.

II Burden of Proof

As noted above, many evidentiary principles relating to burden of proof have been developed in the public international law sphere. These principles are generally applied by investor-state tribunals. This article attempts to illustrate the principles that are most commonly followed, in order to establish an evidentiary framework based on the existing practices of investor-state tribunals.

The principles related to burden of proof illustrate that it is an absolute standard before the ICJ and arbitration tribunals alike. While there are slightly diverging areas, the most basic principles related to burden of proof suggest there is coherence in how courts and tribunals have applied it.

1 *Principle #1: A Party That Raises a Particular Issue Has the Burden of Proof*

The general principle that a party who brings up a particular issue is the one who has the burden of proof comes from the Latin phrase "*actori incumbit*

67 *See* The *Norwegian Loans Case*, 1957 ICJ Reports at 39–40 (Judge Lauterpacht, Separate Opinion); *Kenneth P. Yeager Case*, 17 *Iran-US CTR* 108 (1987) ("no unreasonable standards [for burden of proof] may be applied").

68 Riddell & Plant, *supra* note 17, at 123.

onus probandi".[69] It is not unique to investor-state arbitration, as it comes from legal traditions in Roman, common, and civil law countries.[70] Numerous dispute resolution bodies, including the PCIJ, ICJ, and WTO have recognized this principle.[71] It is a principle required to ensure a fair trial,[72] as it ensures that both claimant and respondent must substantiate any factual allegations made.[73]

1.1 Development of Case Law in PCIJ/ICJ

The PCIJ recognized this principle as early as 1925 in the *Mavrommatis Jerusalem Concessions* case. There, the party who put forth the allegation that he was an Ottoman subject was the one who had to prove his nationality.[74] This understanding has continued to develop throughout the life of the PCIJ. In 1933, for example, the Court ruled that "[i]f it is alleged by one of the Parties

69 Some refer to this Latin maxim as *onus probandi actori incumbit, onus probandi,* or *actori incumbit probation*—all these variations refer to the same principle. KAZAZI, *supra* note 23, at 36; AMERASINGHE, *supra* note 1 at 61–62.

70 CHENG, *supra* note 17 at 327 ("With regard to the incidence of the burden of proof in particular, international judicial decisions are not wanting which expressly hold that there exists a general principle of law placing the burden of proof upon the claimant and that this principle is applicable to international judicial proceedings. In *The Queen Case* (1872), for instance, it was held that:- 'One must follow, as a general rule of solution, the principle of jurisprudence accepted by the law of all countries, that it is for the claimant to make the proof of his claim'."). *See also* MANI, *supra* note 22; KAZAZI, *supra* note 24, at 51; AMERASINGHE, *supra* note 1 at 61–62; RIDDELL & PLANT, *supra* note 17, at 87; WAINCYMER, *supra* note 17 at 762–64 (2012).

71 *See* Riddell, supra note 17, ("Since Roman times, courts of law have relied on the maxim *actori incumbit onus probandi* or "the claimant carries the burden of proof ... [d]espite a variety of approaches and differences of opinions as to the degree of applicability of the rule, various international adjudicative bodies, including several arbitral tribunals, the PCIJ, the ICJ, and human rights bodies have consistently applied the *actori incumbit probatio* rule."); *Reza Said Malek v The Government of the Islamic Republic of Iran*, Case No 193, Award No 534-193-3 (Aug. 11, 1992), *in* Albert Jan van den Berg (ed.), Yearbook Commercial Arbitration, vol. XVIII, at 289 (1993) (Iran-US Claims Tribunal stating that "[i]t goes without saying that it is the Claimant who carries the initial burden of proving the facts upon which he relies."); Netherlands Arbitration Institute (NAI) Case No 3702, Final Award 37 (2011) (unpublished) ("In the Tribunal's view Claimant has done nothing more than articulate the usual burden of proof Standard, i.e. that Claimant must prove its claims and, if it does, Respondent bears the burden of proving its defenses."); *Application of the Convention on the Prevention and Punishment of the Crime of Genocide* (*Croatia v Serbia*), Judgment, ICJ Reports 2015 ¶ 172 (Feb. 3, 2015).

72 AMERASINGHE, *supra* note 1 at 34, 61, 88.

73 O'MALLEY, *supra* note 28, at 203.

74 *Mavrommatis Jerusalem Concessions*, PCIJ 5 Series A No. 25, at 6 (1925).

that some unusual or exceptional meaning is to be attributed to it, it lies on that Party to establish its contention."[75] The purpose of this rule is to ensure that parties bear responsibility for the allegations that they make.

The ICJ has gone on to recognize this principle as well. The court explicitly stated in the *Case Concerning the Temple of Preah Vihear* that:

> As concerns the burden of proof, it must be pointed out that though, from a formal standpoint, Cambodia is the plaintiff, having instituted the proceedings, Thailand also is a claimant because of the claim which was presented by her in the second Submission of the Counter-Memorial and which relates to the sovereignty over the same piece of territory. Both Cambodia and Thailand base their respective claims on a series of facts and contentions which are asserted or put forward by one party or the other. The burden of proof in respect of these will of course lie on the Party asserting them or putting them forward.[76]

The court cites no rule or case law, suggesting that it is a widely accepted and basic evidentiary principle. Numerous ICJ decisions have repeated this principle with acceptance.[77]

In practice, this principle encounters some difficulties. First, distinguishing between which party is the claimant and respondent for a particular proposed allegation can be challenging.[78] This is especially true when pleadings are simultaneously submitted to the court or tribunal. Simultaneous written

---

75 *Legal Status of Eastern Greenland*, PCIJ 49 Series A/B (1933).

76 *Case Concerning the Temple of Preah Vihear* (*Cambodia v Thailand*), Merits, [1962] ICJ Rep 6, 15–16 (1962).

77 *See Case Concerning Military and Paramilitary Activities In and Against Nicaragua* (*Nicaragua v USA*), Judgment on Jurisdiction and Admissibility, [1984] ICJ Rep 392, at 101 (1984) ("Ultimately, however, it is the litigant seeking to establish a fact who bears the burden of proving it …"); *Case Concerning Oil Platforms* (*Iran v USA*), Judgment, [2003] ICJ Rep 161, at 57 (2003) ("the Court has simply to determine whether the United States has demonstrated that it was the victim of an 'armed attack' by Iran such as to justify it using armed force in self-defence; and the burden of proof of the facts showing the existence of such an attack rests on the United States."); *Case Concerning Avena and Other Mexican Nationals* (*Mexico v USA*), Judgment, [2004] ICJ Rep 12, at 55 (2004) ("Both parties recognize the well-settled principle in international law that a litigant seeking to establish the existence of a fact bears the burden of proving it."); *Case Concerning Application of the Convention of the Prevention and Punishment of the Crime of Genocide* (*Bosnia and Herzegovina v Serbia and Montenegro*), Judgment, [2007] ICJ Rep 43, at 204 (2007) ("On the burden or onus of proof, it is well established in general that the applicant must establish its case and that a party asserting a fact must establish it …").

78 AMERASINGHE, *supra* note 1 at 90–95.

submissions have occurred in numerous cases, which in turn causes challenges in deciding which party was the one to put forth the claim.[79] Other difficulties establishing a standard for burden of proof are due to variations on the subject-matter of the dispute, as well as the nature and types of facts needed.[80]

Cases brought forth by Special Agreement between parties, for instance, can result in this type of ambiguity. In the *Minquiers and Ecrehos* case, the ICJ presided over a dispute over sovereignty of certain rocks and islets between France and the United Kingdom.[81] A Special Agreement made by the parties provided that written proceedings would be "without prejudice to any question of the burden of proof".[82] In this scenario, the Court still held that each party was required to "prove its alleged title and the facts upon which it relies", and that "restricting the application of [this] established rule" would be granted only if a party set forth proof that "such a restriction is valid."[83]

Another issue with this principle is that parties generally have a duty to cooperate with international tribunals to establish the truth in a case anyways.[84] This duty suggests that parties who do not bear the burden still may end up contributing in order to fulfill their duty of cooperation. This duty to cooperate has been recognized by ICJ tribunals specifically.[85]

---

79 *See Standard Chartered Bank v United Republic of Tanzania*, ICSID Case. No. ARB/10/12, Award 7 (Nov. 2, 2012) ("The Parties filed simultaneous Post-Hearing Briefs on 27 January 2012, and simultaneous Reply Post-Hearing Briefs on 27 February 2012."); *Abaclat and Others v Argentine Republic*, ICSID Case No ARB/07/5, Recommendation Pursuant to the Request by ICSID, at 5 (Dec. 19, 2011) ("Both parties are invited to simultaneously file, within two weeks from the date of any explanations ..."); *BSG Resources Limited, BSG Resources (Guinea) Limited, and BSG Resources (Guinea) SARL v Republic of Guinea*, ICSID Case No ARB/14/22, Procedural Order 1 and 5 Consolidation, at 11 (Feb. 14, 2016) (listing "Simultaneous Post-Hearing Memorials" and "Simultaneous Cost Submissions" for submission by both parties); ACP *Axos Capital GmbH v Republic of Kosovo*, ICSID Case No ARB/15/22, Procedural Order No. 1, at 9 (February 10, 2016) ("Electronic versions of communications ordered by the Tribunal to be filed simultaneously shall be transmitted to the Tribunal Secretary only, who shall send them to the opposing party and the Tribunal").

80 *Ahmadou Sadio Diallo* (*Republic of Guinea v Democratic Republic of the Congo*), Merits, Judgment, ICJ Reports 2010 (II) ¶ 54 (2010) ("[t]he determination of the burden of proof is in reality dependent on the subject-matter and the nature of [the] dispute brought before the Court; it varies according to the type of facts which it is necessary to establish for the purposes of the decision of the case.").

81 *Minquiers and Ecrehos* (France/United Kingdom), 1953 ICJ Rep. 47 (Judgment of November 17).

82 *Id.* at 49.

83 *Id.* at 52, 99.

84 AMERASINGHE, *supra* note 1 at 90–95.

85 *Application of the Convention on the Prevention and Punishment of the Crime of Genocide (Croatia v Serbia)*, Judgment, ICJ Reports 2015, at ¶ 173 (citing *Pulp Mills on the River*

1.2 Investor-State Tribunal Application

Investor-state tribunals have generally followed ICJ precedent and applied this burden of proof principle.[86] While some ICSID tribunals have only generally spoken about "following established international law rules" when it related to burden of proof,[87] other tribunals have been more explicit.[88]

In the seminal *Asian Agricultural Products Ltd v Sri Lanka* ruling, the tribunal summarized the rules relating to burden of proof "following established international law rules" in two rules:[89]

> Rule (G)—"There exists a general principle of law placing the burden of proof upon the claimant".
> Rule (H)—"The term actor in the principle *onus probandi actori incumbit* is not to be taken to mean the plaintiff from the procedural standpoint, but the real claimant in view of the issues involved". Hence, with regard to "the proof of individual allegations advanced by the parties in the

---

Uruguay (*Argentina v Uruguay*), Judgment, ICJ Reports 2010 (I) ¶ 163 (2010)) ("Whilst the burden of proof rests in principle on the party which alleges a fact, this does not relieve the other party of its duty to cooperate 'in the provision of such evidence as may be in its possession that could assist the Court in resolving the dispute submitted to it'").

86 *Feldman v Mexico* (*AF*), Award ¶ 177 (Dec. 16, 2002); *Soufraki v UAE*, Award ¶ 58.81 (July 7, 2004); *International Thunderbird Gaming Corp v United Mexican States*, UNCITRAL, Award ¶ 95 (Jan. 26, 2006); *Saipem v Bangladesh*, Decision on Jurisdiction ¶ 83 (March 21, 2007). *See also* CHRISTOPH H. SCHREUER ET AL, THE ICSID CONVENTION: A COMMENTARY 669 (2009) ("ICSID tribunals have applied several rules regarding the burden of proof considering facts upon which the parties rely. These rules are well established in international adjudication. The rules are as follows: · normally the burden of proof is with the claimant; · the burden of proof lies with the party asserting a fact, whether it is the claimant or the respondent.") (bullet points in original).

87 *Asian Agricultural Products Ltd v Republic of Sri Lanka*, ICSID Case No ARB/87/3, Final Award 56 (June 27, 1990).

88 *See Tokios Tokelės v Ukraine*, ICSID Case No ARB/02/18, Award (July 26, 2007), ¶ 121 ("the burden of demonstrating the impact of the state action indisputably rests on the Claimant. The principle of *onus probandi actori incumbit*—that a claimant bears the burden of proving its claims—is widely recognized in practice before international tribunals."); *Middle East Cement Shipping and Handling Co SA v Arab Republic of Egypt*, ICSID Case No ARB/99/6, Award (April 12, 2002), ¶ 89 ("The respective provisions of the BIT confirm what can be considered as a general principle of international procedure—and probably also of virtually all national procedural laws—namely that it is the Claimant who has the burden of proof for the conditions required in the applicable substantive rules of law to establish the claim.").

89 *Asian Agricultural Products Ltd v Republic of Sri Lanka*, ICSID Case No ARB/87/3, Final Award (June 27, 1990), ¶ 56.

> course of proceedings, the burden of proof rests upon the party alleging the fact".[90]

Similarly, in the *Salini Construttori SpA* case, the tribunal cite to this well-established principle that "it is for a claimant to prove the facts on which it relies in support of his claim—*Actori incumbat probatio*'."[91]

Numerous investor state tribunals have followed this approach as well, including the *Chevron* case, where the tribunal noted:

> As a general rule, the holder of a right raising a claim on the basis of that right in legal proceedings bears the burden of proof for all elements required for the claim. However, an exception to this rule occurs when a respondent raises a defense to the effect that the claim is precluded despite the normal conditions being met. In that case, the respondent must assume the burden of proof for the elements necessary for the exception to be allowed.[92]

---

90 *Asian Agricultural Products Ltd v Republic of Sri Lanka*, ICSID Case No ARB/87/3, Final Award (June 27, 1990), ¶ 56. *See also Chevron Corp and Texaco Petroleum Corp v Republic of Ecuador*, UNCITRAL, PCA Case No 34877, Interim Award 139 (1 December 2008) ("The nature of these defenses as exceptions to a general rule that lead to the reversal of the burden of proof stem from, among other factors, the presumption of good faith. A claimant is not required to prove that its claim is asserted in a non-abusive manner; it is for the respondent to raise and prove an abuse as a defense. A respondent whose defense overcomes the presumption of good faith reveals the hierarchy between these norms, as even a well-founded claim will be rejected by the tribunal if it is found to be abusive.").

91 *Salini Construttori SpA and Italstrade SpA v Hashemite Kingdom of Jordan*, ICSID Case No ARB/02/13, Award 70 (January 31, 2006).

92 *Chevron Corp and Texaco Petroleum Corp v Republic of Ecuador*, UNCITRAL, PCA Case No 34877, Interim Award 138 (December 1, 2008). See also *Waguih Elie George Siag and Clorinda Vecchi v The Arab Republic of Egypt*, ICSID Case No ARB/05/15, Award 315 (June 1, 2009) ("As to the burden of proof, the general rule, well established in international arbitrations, is that the Claimant bears the burden of proof with respect to the facts it alleges and the Respondent carries the burden of proof with respect to its defences."); *Saipem SpA v The People's Republic of Bangladesh*, ICSID Case No ARB/05/7, Award 113 (June 30, 2009) ("It is a well-established rule in international adjudication that the burden of proof lies with the party alleging a fact, whether it is the claimant or the respondent."); *RosInvestCo UK Ltd v The Russian Federation*, SCC Case No V079/2005, Final Award 250 (September 12, 2010) ("the Tribunal notes that the Parties seem to agree on the principle that the burden of proof generally lies with the Claimant to establish the facts on which the claim is based. The Tribunal confirms that view and only adds that, however, the burden of proof can shift to the Respondent with regard to any exception on which the Respondent relies in its defence."); *Alpha Projektholding Gmbh v Ukraine*, ICSID Case No ARB/07/16, Award 236 (November 8, 2010) ("The Tribunal agrees with the standard articulated by the AAPL tribunal that, with regard to 'proof of individual allegations advanced by the

The tribunal explains that this principle has been derived from the PCIJ, where the court applied this principle on numerous occasions.[93]

The tribunal in the *Rompetrol* case provided a detailed exposition of the burden of proof in investor-state arbitration:

> [T]he Tribunal finds that it can safely rest, so far as the burden of proof is concerned, on the widely accepted international principle that a party in litigation bears the burden of proving the facts relied on to support its claim or defence. This is often put as a maxim: he who asserts must prove (*onus probandi incumbit actori*). A claimant before an international tribunal must establish the facts on which it bases its case or else it will lose the arbitration. The respondent does not in that sense bear any "burden of proof" of its own, but if it fails where necessary to throw sufficient doubt

---

parties in the course of proceedings, the burden of proof rests upon the party alleging the fact.'"); *Vito G. Gallo v The Government of Canada*, UNCITRAL, PCA Case No 55798, Award 277 (September 15, 2011) ("the principle actori incumbit probatio is a coin with two sides: the Claimant has to prove its case, and without evidence it will fail; but if the Respondent raises defences, of fraud or otherwise, the burden shifts, and the defences can only succeed if supported by evidence marshalled by the Respondent."); *Société Générale de Surveillance S.A. v The Republic of Paraguay*, ICSID Case No ARB/07/29, Award 79 (February 10, 2012) [79] ("Claimant bears the initial burden of proof in substantiating its claims, and Respondent bears the burden of proving its defenses."); *Churchill Mining PLC and Planet Mining Pty Ltd v Republic of Indonesia*, ICSID Case No ARB/12/14 and 12/40, Award 238 (December 6, 2016) ("Starting with the burden of proof, the Tribunal deems it appropriate to apply international law to this issue, since the claims brought in this arbitration seek to establish the responsibility of a State for breach of the latter's international obligations. It is a well-established rule in international law that each Party bears the burden of proving the facts which it alleges (actori incumbit onus probandi). Since the Respondent alleges that the Survey and Exploration Licenses and related documents are forged and that the Exploitation Licenses were obtained through deception, the Respondent bears the burden of proving its allegations of forgery and deception.").

93 *See, e.g.*, *Pac Rim Cayman LLC v Republic of El Salvador*, ICSID Case No ARB/09/12, Decision on Jurisdictional Objections ¶ 2.11 (June 1, 2012) ("As far as the burden of proof is concerned, in the Tribunal's view, it cannot here be disputed that the party which alleges something positive has ordinarily to prove it to the satisfaction of the Tribunal."); *Bernhard von Pezold and others v Republic of Zimbabwe*, ICSID Case No ARB/10/15, Award ¶ 174 (July 28, 2015) ("The general rule is that the party asserting the claim bears the burden of establishing it by proof. Where claims and counterclaims go to the same factual issue, each party bears the burden of proof as to its own contentions. There is no general notion of shifting of the burden of proof when jurisdictional objections are asserted. The Respondent in this case therefore bears the burden of proving its objections. Conversely, the Claimants must prove any facts asserted in response to the Respondent's objections and bear the overall burden of establishing that jurisdiction exists.").

> on the claimant's factual premises, it runs the risk in turn of losing the arbitration; but only 'the risk,' because the particular factual premise may not in the event turn out to be decisive in the legal analysis. Conversely, if the respondent chooses to put forward fresh allegations of its own in order to counter or undermine the claimant's case, then by doing so the respondent takes upon itself the burden of proving what it has alleged.[94]

Ad hoc tribunals in investor-state arbitrations that followed the UNCITRAL Rules also ruled similarly. When the claimant is the party that alleges certain facts, the claimant is the party who holds the burden of proof.[95] The reverse, therefore, is true for a respondent that alleges any facts—it will then be the party who holds the burden of proof.[96] In the investor-state context, a respondent may challenge a tribunal's jurisdiction or raise certain defenses—here, the respondent has the burden of proof.

2 *Principle #2: Burden of Proof Will Not Be Relaxed*

2.1 Development of Case Law in PCIJ/ICJ

Various circumstances may arise that cause a party to have difficulty in meeting their burden of proof. For example, hardships in obtaining evidence or limited access to documentation can lead to insufficient presentation of evidence. In these cases, the ICJ has not shown any leniency in the burden of proof standard.

The *Avena* case was explicit that difficulties in obtaining evidence was no excuse for shifting the burden of proof. In *Avena*, the United States argued that pertinent information regarding citizenship was held by the Mexican government and thus, should be Mexico's burden to prove.[97] The court disagreed and ruled that the United States was the party that should have sought the information from Mexico and was also the party responsible for "furnish[ing] the

94 *The Rompetrol Group NV v Romania*, ICSID Case No ARB/06/3, Award ¶ 179 (May 6, 2013).

95 *CME Czech Republic BV (The Netherlands) v The Czech Republic*, UNCITRAL, Partial Award ¶ 285 (Sept. 13, 2001) ("In respect to the breach of the Treaty as alleged, the burden of proof is on the Claimant to demonstrate that both the breach and the responsibility of the Czech State is engaged.").

96 *See, e.g., Vito G Gallo v Government of Canada*, UNCITRAL, PCA Case No 55798, Award ¶ 277 (Sept. 15, 2011) ("the principle *actori incumbit probatio* is a coin with two sides: the Claimant has to prove its case, and without evidence it will fail; but if the Respondent raises defences, of fraud or otherwise, the burden shifts, and the defences can only succeed if supported by evidence marshalled by the Respondent.").

97 *Avena, supra* note 77, at ¶ 56.

Court with all information on the matter."[98] Because the United States failed to produce the evidence, the burden of proof was not met.[99]

Similarly, the ICJ court in a border dispute case acknowledged the difficulties in providing evidence of human settlement within a disputed area.[100] However, when no more than a few birth and death records and military records with no border or specific location descriptions were produced as evidence, the tribunal found that the burden was not met.[101] Other border dispute cases, like *Cameroon v Nigeria*, found in a similar way. Despite difficulties in procuring evidence, the Court stated that any allegations that were unproven by the party submitting the allegation would be rejected.[102]

More recently, in *Croatia v Serbia*, a party presented documentary evidence that included unsigned statements because of difficulties it had with obtaining evidence.[103] Although the court accepted the admissibility of the evidence, it treated the statements "with caution", as per previous ICJ judgments.[104] Still, in the judgment, the court noted that these unsigned statements were "deficient" for various reasons and did not accord any evidential weight to the statements that were unsigned nor unconfirmed by other credible evidence.[105] Even though the court had acknowledged difficulties involved in obtaining evidence, it was not possible to use that defense to alleviate a party's burden of proof.

2.2 Investor-State Tribunal Application

Investor-state tribunals have applied this principle in its cases as well.[106] Regardless of how much effort was put into obtaining evidence, being unsuccessful in proving the burden results in the court finding for the opposing party.

98 *Id.* at ¶ 57.

99 *Id.*

100 *Land, Island and Maritime Frontier Dispute* (*El Salvador/Honduras: Nicaragua intervening*), ICJ Judgment 470 (Sept. 11, 1992).

101 *Id.* at 470–479.

102 *Land and Maritime Boundary between Cameroon and Nigeria* (*Cameroon v Nigeria: Equatorial Guinea intervening*), Judgment, 2002 ICJ Reports 303, 453 (Oct. 10, 2002).

103 *Application of the Convention on the Prevention and Punishment of the Crime of Genocide* (*Croatia v Serbia*), Judgment, ICJ Reports 2015, at 77–78 (2015).

104 *Id.; See also Territorial and Maritime Dispute between Nicaragua and Honduras in the Caribbean Sea* (*Nicaragua v Honduras*), Judgment, ICJ Reports 2007 (II) ¶ 244 (2007).

105 *Application of the Convention on the Prevention and Punishment of the Crime of Genocide* (*Croatia v Serbia*), Judgment, ICJ Reports 2015 at 78–79.

106 *See Military and Paramilitary Activities In and Against Nicaragua* (*Nicaragua v USA*) (Jurisdiction and Admissibility, Judgment) [1984] ICJ Rep 392 at 101 ("Ultimately, however, it is the litigant seeking to establish a fact who bears the burden of proving it; and in cases

This situation occurred in *Al-Bahoul v Tajikstan*, where the Claimant was unable to access evidence located in Tajikstan.[107] When the sovereign state controls the evidence, a Claimant may rely on inferences and circumstantial evidence, but a tribunal will not shift the burden of proof.[108] The tribunal in *Al-Bahoul* explained:

> Claimant has represented to the Tribunal that extensive efforts were made to obtain further documentary evidence in support of his case, but were not successful since such evidence is located in Tajikistan where Claimant and his representatives no longer have access to it. While the Tribunal can understand that currently Claimant may have no or very limited access to documents in Tajikistan, this does not allow the Tribunal to make far-reaching assumptions to the detriment of Respondent.

In these types of circumstances, tribunals must take great care. As one tribunal warns in the *Lao Holdings* case:

> The Tribunal notes the Claimant's contention that against a sovereign state a Claimant "is often unable to furnish direct proof of facts giving rise to responsibility" because, as the Claimant argues, such evidence is often "exclusively within the control of the Government." Nevertheless where, as here, the Claimant's case is based on "inferences of fact and circumstantial evidence" ... a Tribunal must be careful not to shift the onus of proof from the Claimant to the Respondent Government or to bend over backwards to read in inferences against "the sovereign state" that are simply not justified in the context of the whole case.[109]

---

where evidence may not be forthcoming, a submission may in the judgment be rejected as unproved ...").

107 *Mohammad Ammar Al-Bahloul v Republic of Tajikstan*, SCC Case No V (064/2008), Partial Award on Jurisdiction and Liability ¶ 115 (Sept. 2, 2009).

108 See, e.g., RICHARD M. MOSK, THE ROLE OF FACTS IN INTERNATIONAL DISPUTE RESOLUTION 136 (Recueil des cours 2003) ("The Rule that the burden of proof lies on him who affirms a fact and not on him who denies it (*ei qui affirmat. non ei qui negat incumbit probantio*) admits of no exception—none whatsoever. Nor is there any room under the Rule for a shift in the burden of proof at any of the middle stages of the proceeding. Throughout the case and at the end of the day, the duty to prove an asserted fact remains with him who makes it. In the absence of satisfactory proof on his part, he can never succeed in his assertion on the basis of his adversary's failure to carry a shifted burden'."); *Lao Holdings NV v Lao People's Democratic Republic*, ICSID Case No ARB(AF)/12/6, Decision on the Merits ¶ 11 (June 10, 2015).

109 *Lao Holdings v Lao*, ICSID Case No ARB(AF)/12/6, at ¶ 11.

This principle is also clearly stated by the annulment committee in *Azurix v Argentina*. When Argentina contended that a better-positioned party to prove a fact is the one that bears the burden of proof, the annulment committee rejected the notion, noting that:

> In its letter dated August 2, 2004, Argentina refers to what it claims is "a general principle of law that the party that is in a better position to prove a fact bears the burden of proof". The Committee does not accept that such general principle exists in ICSID proceedings: to the contrary, the Committee considers the general principle in ICSID proceedings, and in international adjudication generally, to be that "who asserts must prove", and that in order to do so, the party which asserts must itself obtain and present the necessary evidence in order to prove what it asserts.[110]

This statement recognizably does not preclude a party from making a motion seeking documents at the production phase of the hearing, if permitted. Once the merits are being adjudicated by the tribunal, however, there will be no burden shifting or relaxation of the burden.

3 *Principle #3: At the Jurisdictional Phase, the Burden of Proof Follows the* "pro tem" *Principle*

The question of whether a party has met its burden of proof depends heavily on which standard of proof is used. A unique situation arises when discussing burden of proof during the jurisdictional phase. At this preliminary phase, relevant facts and arguments that implicate the merits phase are not yet made.[111] However, it is crucial that a party meet its burden of proof in establishing jurisdiction of the tribunal. This requirement necessitates that some relevant facts regarding the merits of the case are, at a minimum, raised during this phase.

3.1 Development of Case Law in PCIJ/ICJ

The ICJ applies the *pro tem* rule, analogous to a *prima facie* requirement at the jurisdictional stage, where, first, claimants must allege facts that are sufficient

---

110 *Azurix Corp v Argentine Republic*, ICSID Case No ARB/01/12, Decision on the Application for Annulment of Argentine Republic ¶ 215 (Sept. 1, 2009).

111 *Plama Consortium Ltd v Republic of Bulgaria*, ICSID Case No ARB/03/24, Decision on Jurisdiction 167 (Feb. 8, 2005) ("In the Tribunal's view, as already indicated above, the burden of proof on the merits is significantly different from the burden applied to a jurisdictional issue.").

to find a legal dispute arising from the circumstances.[112] This principle was set forth in the *Oil Platforms* case by Judge Higgins:

> The only way in which, in the present case, it can be determined whether the claims of Iran are sufficiently plausibly … is to accept pro tem the facts as alleged by Iran to be true … for jurisdictional purposes—that is to say, to see if on the basis of Iran's claims of fact there could occur a violation of one or more of them.[113]

It is commonly understood that the sufficiently plausible facts alleged by Claimant will be accepted as true during the jurisdictional phase.[114] This is despite the fact that the ICJ on one occasion stated that the evidence submitted in the jurisdictional phase does not yet have to be proven by either party.[115] However, subsequent ICJ decisions have reiterated the *pro tem* rule.[116] This is because the facts that relate to the merits can be proven appropriately at the merits phase, should the case proceed to the merits phase. At the jurisdictional phase, the Court needs to be only satisfied that the merits allegations would fall within its jurisdiction.

---

112 *See Oil Platforms (Iran v USA)*, [1996] ICJ Rep 847, at ¶ 32–34 (Dec. 12, 1996) (Separate Opinion of Judge Higgins).

113 *Id.* at ¶ 32.

114 *Id.*

115 *Fisheries Jurisdiction (Spain v Canada)*, Judgment, [1998] ICJ Reports 432, at ¶¶ 37–38 (1998) ("The Court points out that the establishment or otherwise of jurisdiction is not a matter for the parties but for the Court itself. Although a party seeking to assert a fact must bear the burden of proving it (see Military and Paramilitary Activities in and against Nicaragua (Nicaragua v United States of America), Jurisdiction and Admissibility, Judgment I.C.J. Reports 1984, p. 437, para. 101), this has no relevance for the establishment of the Court's jurisdiction, which is a "question of law to be resolved in the light of the relevant facts" (Border and Transborder Armed Actions (Nicaragua v Honduras), Jurisdiction and Admissibility, Judgment, I.C.J. Reports 1988, p. 76, para. 16). That being so, there is no burden of proof to be discharged in the matter of jurisdiction. Rather, it is for the Court to determine from all the facts and taking into account all the arguments advanced by the Parties, "whether the force of the arguments militating in favour of jurisdiction is preponderant, and to 'ascertain whether an intention on the part of the Parties exists to confer jurisdiction upon it'"…).

116 *See, e.g., Legality of Use of Force (Yugoslavia v Italy)*, Request for the Indication of Provisional Measures, [1999] ICJ Reports 481, at 25 (1998) ("[T]he Court must ascertain whether the breaches of the Convention alleged by Yugoslavia are capable of falling within the provisions of that instrument and whether, as a consequence, the dispute is one which the Court has jurisdiction *ratione materiae* to entertain pursuant to Article IX …").

3.2 Investor-State Tribunal Application

The *pro tem* rule expounded by the ICJ has been followed in the investor-state context as well for resolving jurisdictional issues. Indeed, invoking jurisdiction in an investor-state context is also unique in itself. An investor party must be able to show that the host state has consented to arbitrate the dispute as well as whether the specific dispute falls within the boundaries of a bilateral investment treaty (BIT) or multilateral investment treaty (MIT).[117] Without this showing, a tribunal would not have jurisdiction to act in resolving the dispute. These two preconditions to fulfilling jurisdiction require submitting evidence and meeting the Claimant's burden of proof. Without submitting pertinent evidence to fulfill these preconditions, a tribunal could not proceed in adjudicating the dispute.

Investor-state tribunals have adopted the *pro tem* standard, citing and interpreting the *Oil Platforms* principle regarding jurisdictional burden of proof favorably.[118] The *pro tem* rule is generally confined to whether a claimant can meet the jurisdiction requirements fully. Any factual questions relating to a tribunal's jurisdiction no longer applies the *pro tem* or *prima facie* standard,

117 *See, e.g., Phoenix Action Ltd v Czech Republic,* ICSID Case No ARB/06/5, Award (April 15, 2009) ¶ 54; *Mobil Corp, Venezuela Holdings BV v Bolivarian Republic of Venezuela,* ICSID Case No ARB/07/27, Decision on Jurisdiction (June 10, 2010), ¶¶ 138, 140; *Hussein Nuaman Soufraki v United Arab Emirates,* ICSID Case No ARB/02/7, Decision of the ad hoc Committee on the Application for Annulment of Mr Soufraki ¶ 76 (June 5, 2007).

118 *See, e.g., Methanex Corp v United States,* UNCITRAL, Partial Award ¶ 116 (August 7, 2002); *SGS Société Générale de Surveillance SA v Republic of the Philippines,* ICSID Case No ARB/02/6, Decision of the Tribunal on Objections to Jurisdiction ¶ 26 (January 29, 2004); *Salini Construttori SpA and Italstrade SpA v Hashemite Kingdom of Jordan,* ICSID Case No ARB/02/13, Decision on Jurisdiction ¶¶ 139–51 (Nov. 9, 2004); *Plama Consortium,* at 119; *Desert Line Projects LLC v Republic of Yemen,* ICSID Case No ARB/05/17, Award ¶ 129 (February 6, 2008); *Pac Rim Cayman LLC v Republic of El Salvador,* ICSID Case No ARB/09/12, Decision on the Respondent's Jurisdictional Objections ¶ 2.5 (June 1, 2012) ("('At an early jurisdictional stage of an arbitration, as regards facts alleged by a claimant in its pleadings but not admitted or even denied by a respondent, the Tribunal acknowledges that it is often said that an arbitration tribunal is required to test the factual basis of claimant's claim by reference only to a 'prima facie' standard—as regards the merits of such claim. That standard was most clearly expressed by Judge Higgins in the well-known passage from her separate opinion in Oil Platforms; and it has been applied, as a general practice, by many tribunals in applying jurisdictional objections made in many investor-state arbitrations"); *Noble Energy Inc. and Machala Power Cia Ltda v Ecuador and Consejo Nacional de Electricidad,* ICSID Case No ARB/05/12, Decision on Jurisdiction ¶¶ 151–152 (Mar. 5, 2008) ("the Tribunal will assess for each claim if the facts alleged may be capable, *if proved,* of constituting breaches of the BIT"); *BP American Production Company & Ors v Argentina,* ICSID Case No ARB/04/8, Decision on Preliminary Objections ¶¶ 47–51 (July 27, 2006).

and a party must prove the jurisdictional issue appropriately in this analysis. These factual questions may also include those pertaining to abuse of process, *ratione temporis*, and denial of benefits.[119]

A number of investor-state tribunals have adopted this *prima facie* approach for their analysis in granting a party success in making their jurisdictional claim.[120] However, some tribunals also warned against a formalized rule when the circumstances may dictate otherwise.[121]

---

119 *Pac Rim Cayman LLC v Republic of El Salvador*, ICSID Case No ARB/09/12, Decision on the Respondent's Jurisdictional Objections ¶¶ 2.8–2.9 (June 1, 2012) ("[T]he Tribunal considers that it is impermissible for the Tribunal to found its jurisdiction on any of the Claimant's CAFTA claims on the basis of an assumed fact (i.e. alleged by the Claimant in its pleadings as regards jurisdiction but disputed by the Respondent). The application of that "prima facie" or other like standard is limited to testing the merits of a claimant's case at a jurisdictional stage; and it cannot apply to a factual issue upon which a tribunal's jurisdiction directly depends, such as the Abuse of Process, Ratione Temporis and Denial of Benefits issues in this case. In the context of factual issues which are common to both jurisdictional issues and the merits, there could be, of course, no difficulty in joining the same factual issues to the merits. That, however, is not the situation here, where a factual issue relevant only to jurisdiction and not to the merits requires more than a decision pro tempore by a tribunal.… Accordingly, this Tribunal is here required to determine finally whether it has jurisdiction over the Claimant's CAFTA claims on the proven existence of certain facts because all relevant facts supporting such jurisdiction must be established by the Claimant at this jurisdictional stage and not merely assumed in the Claimant's favour.").

120 *See, e.g., Amco v Indonesia*, Decision on Jurisdiction ¶ 38 (Sept. 25, 1983); *Maffezini v Spain*, Decision on Jurisdiction ¶ 69 (Jan. 25, 2000); *SGS v Pakistan*, Decision on Jurisdiction ¶¶ 1–15 (Aug. 6, 2003); *Azurix v Argentina*, Decision on Jurisdiction ¶ 76 (Dec. 8, 2003); *SGS v Philippines*, Decision on Jurisdiction ¶ 26 (January 29, 2004); *Siemens v Argentina*, Decision on Jurisdiction ¶ 180 (August 3, 2004); *Joy Mining v Egypt*, Award ¶¶ 29–30 (Aug. 6, 2004); *Salini v Jordan*, Decision on Jurisdiction ¶ 151 (Nov. 29, 2004); *Plama v Bulgaria*, Decision on Jurisdiction ¶¶ 118–120, 132 (Feb. 8, 2005); *Impregilo v Pakistan*, Decision on Jurisdiction ¶¶ 230, 237–254 (April 22, 2005); *Bayindir v Pakistan*, Decision on Jurisdiction ¶¶ 185–200 (Nov. 14, 2005); *Duke Energy v Peru*, Decision on Jurisdiction ¶ 87 (Feb. 1, 2006); *Continental Casualty v Argentina*, Decision on Jurisdiction ¶ 59–64 (Feb. 22, 2006); *El Paso v Argentina*, Decision on Jurisdiction ¶¶ 40–45, 109 (April 27, 2006); *Jan de Nul v Egypt*, Decision on Jurisdiction ¶¶ 69–71 (June 16, 2006); *LESI & Astaldi v Alergia*, Decision on Jurisdiction ¶ 84iv (July 12, 2006); *Pan American v Argentina*, Decision on Preliminary Objections ¶¶ 43–51, 131 (July 27, 2006); *Total v Argentina*, Decision on Jurisdiction ¶¶ 52–55 (August 25, 2006); *Telenor v Hungary*, Award ¶¶ 34, 53, 68, 80 (Sept. 13, 2006); *Helnan v Egypt*, Decision on Jurisdiction ¶¶ 73, 81, 91, 94 (Oct. 17, 2006); *Saipem v Bangladesh*, Decision on Jurisdiction ¶¶ 83–91, 129–134, 144–147, 149 (Mar. 21, 2007); *Siag v Egypt*, Decision on Jurisdiction ¶¶ 139–141 (April 11, 2007); *Kardassopoulos v Georgia*, Decision on Jurisdiction ¶¶ 103–104 (July 6, 2007); *MCI v Ecuador*, Award ¶¶ 162–163 (July 31, 2007).

121 *See, e.g., CMS Gas Transmission Co v Argentine Republic*, ICSID Case No ARB/01/8, Decision of the Tribunal on Objections to Jurisdiction ¶ 35 (July 17, 2003) ("For the time being, the fact that the Claimant has demonstrated *prima facie* that it has been adversely affected by measures adopted by the Republic of Argentina is sufficient for the Tribunal to

The *Hamester v Ghana* tribunal explains the burden of proof between the jurisdictional and merits phase aptly:

> In order to clarify the distinction between a jurisdictional question and a merits question, it is useful to consider the different burden of proof required for each. If jurisdiction rests on the existence of certain facts, they have to be proven at the jurisdictional stage. However, if facts are alleged in order to establish a violation of the relevant BIT, they have to be accepted as such at the jurisdictional stage, until their existence is ascertained (or not) at the merits stage.[122]

Thus, many investor-state tribunals have still required a fulfillment of the jurisdictional burden of proof at the jurisdictional phase.[123]

4 *Principle #4: Failure to Meet the Burden of Proof Can Lead to Dismissal of That Claim and if the Claim Is Particularly Significant, It Can Be Fatal to the Case*

4.1 Development of Case Law in PCIJ/ICJ

In the 1920s, the PCIJ court issued opinions that implicated the basic principle that failing to meet the burden of proof would result in a dismissal of a claim. In the *Case concerning Certain German interests in Polish Upper Silesia*, a German agent on behalf of claimant made a brief reference in oral proceedings

---

consider that the claim, as far as this matter is concerned, is admissible and that it has jurisdiction to examine it on the merits"); *Emilio Agustín Maffezini v Kingdom of Spain*, ICSID Case No ARB/97/7, Decision of the Tribunal on Objections to Jurisdiction ¶ 70 (Jan. 25, 2000) (same); *PSEG Global Inc, North American Coal Corp, and Konya Ilgin Elektrik Üretim ve Ticaret Limited Sirketi v Republic of Turkey*, ICSID Case No ARB/02/5, Decision on Jurisdiction ¶ 64 (June 4, 2004), (same); *Saipem SpA v People's Republic of Bangladesh*, ICSID Case No ARB/05/7, Decision on Jurisdiction and Recommendation on Provisional Measures ¶ 83 (March 21, 2007).

122 *Gustav F W Hamester GmbH & Co KG v Republic of Ghana*, ICSID Case No ARB/07/24, Award ¶ 143 (June 18, 2010).

123 *Perenco Ecuador Ltd v Republic of Ecuador and Empresa Estatal Petróleos del Ecuador*, ICSID Case No ARB/08/6, Decision on Jurisdiction ¶¶ 97–98 (June 30, 2011), ("Where an investment is owned and/or controlled by the investor/claimant through a series of corporations, typically the claimant will adduce evidence as to how it owns or controls such investment ... The burden of proof to establish the facts supporting its claim to standing lies with the Claimant."); *Abaclat et al v Argentina*, ICSID Case No ARB/07/5, ¶ 678; *Libananco Holdings Co Ltd v Republic of Turkey*, ICSID Case No ARB/06/8, Award (Sept. 2, 2011), ¶ 122; *Caratube International Oil Co LLP v Republic of Kazakhstan*, ICSID Case No ARB/08/12, Award (June 5, 2012), ¶ 367.

without providing any details substantiating his claim.[124] The Court disregarded the claim in this circumstance "for lack of sufficiently substantiated statements."[125] The PCIJ has reiterated this basic principle numerous times in instances where claims are dismissed when a party fails to meet their burden of proof through lack of evidence.[126]

Several reasons underlie why the principle exists. One of the most important reasons is that it notifies parties that a tribunal should not have any procedural duty to inform the parties at each and every stage of the proceedings the risk involved if a party should choose not to produce or submit evidence.[127] With this understanding, parties are bound in bearing the risk of ensuring they submit sufficient evidence to meet the burden of proof.[128]

4.2 Investor-State Tribunal Application

Investor state tribunals generally rule against parties who fail to meet their burden of proof. Most of these cases occur because the party who holds the burden of proof is unable to meet its burden. In circumstances where there is

---

124 *Case concerning certain German interests in Polish Upper Silesia* (The merits), Judgment No. 7, at 65 (May 25, 1926) ("The terse reference, without any details, to subsidence, made by the German Agent in his oral reply, would, even apart from the question whether this argument had been put forward in sufficient time, not suffice to prove the assertion made in the Application. The Respondent has stated that he is not in a position to reply to this argument which was not put forward during the written proceedings. In these circumstances, therefore, the Court can only dismiss the Applicant's claim, for lack of sufficiently substantiated statements.").

125 *Id.*

126 *See Mavrommatis Jerusalem Concessions* (*Greece v U.K.*), 1925 P.C.I.J. (ser. A) No. 5, at 30 (Mar. 26, 1925) ("but no proof that such was actually the standpoint of these authorities has been produced. The contention of the Respondent in regard to this point therefore fails through lack of evidence to support it"); *Jurisdiction of the European Commission of the Danube Between Galatz and Braila*, PCIJ Series B.—No. 14, at 67 (Dec. 8, 1927) ("The absence, however, of findings of pertinent facts of record in respect to this specific point does not suffice to prove that such a right, which is a necessary corollary to the duties of, the European Commission, does not exist."); *Jurisdiction of the European Commission of the Danube Between Galatz and Braila*, PCIJ Series B.—No. 14, at 83 (Dec. 8, 1927) (Opinion of Judge Moore) ("No such proof has been adduced, and to argue that, in its absence, the European Commission now possesses above Galatz no juridical powers, is in effect to maintain that the specific provisions of the Definitive Statute, and of the previous international acts which—it confirms, have been impliedly revoked by what the Interpretative Protocol failed to Say."); *Jurisdiction of the European Commission of the Danube Between Galatz and Braila*, PCIJ Series B.—No. 14, at 125 (Dec. 8, 1927) (Opinion of Judge Negulesco).

127 See O'MALLEY, *supra* note 28, at 206.

128 *Id.*

divergence regarding a factual allegation, the party with the burden of proof must affirmatively prove that allegation for the tribunal to rule in favor of that allegation.[129] ICSID tribunals have repeatedly found this way for both issues dealing with merit and those dealing with jurisdictional questions.[130]

The only instance where a party with the burden of proof does not have to affirmatively prove their allegations is when the truth of the allegation is already within the knowledge of the tribunal, or is presumed by the tribunal.[131]

Even in the jurisdictional phase, a party faces the possibility to not being able to meet their burden of proof when it comes to factual issues involving jurisdiction; a failure to meet their burden results in a fatal case.[132] In the merit

129 *Plama Consortium Ltd v Bulgaria*, ICSID Case No ARB/03/24, Award 248–249 (Aug. 27, 2008).

130 *Plama Consortium*, ICSID Case No ARB/03/24, ¶ 249 ("Given this conflicting evidence, the Arbitral Tribunal is unable to form any firm view as to what really transpired. The burden of proof being on Claimant, the tribunal cannot, therefore, rule in its favor concerning these allegations, including with respect to its claim under Article 12 of the ECT"); *Salini Construttori SpA and Italstrade SpA v Hashemite Kingdom of Jordan*, ICSID Case No ARB/02/13, Award (Jan. 31, 2006), ¶ 163 (rejecting a portion of the claim because Claimant was unable to substantiate their alleged facts when "they present no argument, and no evidence whatsoever, to sustain their treaty Claim and they do not show that the alleged facts are capable of falling within the provisions of Article 2(3). The Tribunal, therefore, has no jurisdiction to consider this first treaty claim."); *Caratube International Oil Co LLP v Republic of Kazakhstan*, ICSID Case No ARB/08/12, Award ¶¶ 457, 468 (June 5, 2012) (failing to discharge burden of proof for jurisdictional matter bars Tribunal from hearing merits of the case); *ICS Inspection and Control Services Ltd v Argentine Republic*, PCA Case No 2010–9, Award on Jurisdiction ¶ 280 (Feb. 10, 2012) ("The burden of proof for the issue of consent falls squarely on a given claimant who invokes it against a given respondent. Where a claimant fails to prove consent with sufficient certainty, jurisdiction will be declined."); *Emmis International Holding, BV, Emmis Radio Operating, BV, MEM Magyar Electronic Media Kereskedelmi és Szolgáltató Kft v Hungary*, ICSID Case No ARB/12/2, Award ¶ 171 (April 16, 2014) ("The Claimants bear the burden of proof. If the Claimants' burden of proving ownership of the claim is not met, the Respondent has no burden to establish the validity of its jurisdictional defences").

131 CHENG, *supra* note 17 at 334–35 ("[T]he burden of proof rests upon the party alleging the fact, unless the truth of the fact is within judicial knowledge or is presumed by the Tribunal.").

132 *Liman Caspian Oil*, ICSID Case No ARB/07/14, at ¶ 194 ("However, the burden of proving fraud and bribery regarding the making of the original investment lies with Respondent. The Tribunal considers that Respondent has not provided sufficient proof for its allegations that the Licence was acquired by fraudulent misrepresentation to the Ministry of Energy and/or by fraud on the minority shareholders. Therefore, the Tribunal concludes that Respondent was not able to satisfy its burden of proof of facts showing a breach of international public policy."); *Teinver SA, Transportes de Cercanías SA and Autobuses Urbanos del Sur SA v Argentine Republic*, ICSID Case No ARB/09/1, Decision on Jurisdiction ¶ 324 (December 21, 2012) ("Respondent has failed to demonstrate that Claimants, as a

adjudication phase especially, failure to meet the burden of proof results in a dismissal of the merits of the case. Further, even in the damages phase of a case, failure to meet the burden of proof is fatal to the case. ICSID tribunals have found that failure to meet the burden of proof during this portion of adjudication results in a finding of no damages.[133]

If a tribunal misapplies the burden of proof principle in any of the procedural, substantive, or damages phases, the result can be an annulment in the award.[134]

III Standard of Proof

The standard of proof in international law is complicated due to a lack of information and standardization, differentiations of standards within common law and civil law systems, and a lack of formal rules surrounding the principle.[135] While there is consensus concerning the fundamental understanding on burden of proof, this is less true for standard of proof.[136]

Throughout its history, ICJ jurisprudence highlights the difficulty of harmonizing various standards of proof.[137] Under the ICJ Statute, Article 53 provides some clarity on evidentiary standards. Article 53 allows a Court to rule in a party's favor when the other party fails to appear or defend its case, but only when the first party has fulfilled its burden on jurisdiction and also shown that their claim is "well founded in fact and law".[138] In practice, ICJ tribunals often do not discuss the standard of proof that shall be applied to the evidence, nor do tribunals usually explain the standard they apply when rendering a

factual matter, committed illegalities in the process of *acquiring* their investment in the Argentine Airlines. In this respect, the onus is on Respondent.").

133 *See Víctor Pey Casado and President Allende Foundation v Republic of Chile*, ICSID Case No ARB/98/2, Award ¶ 234 (September 13, 2016) ("The Tribunal has therefore no option but to find that the Claimants have failed to prove any material injury caused to either of them as the sufficiently direct result of the Respondent's breach of Article 4 of the BIT. The Tribunal cannot therefore, on principle, make any award of damages.").

134 *Caratube International*, ICSID Case No ARB/08/12, at 97 (citing *Klöckner v Republic of Cameroon*, ICSID Case No ARB/81/2, Decision on Annulment (May 3, 1985) ("a reversal of the burden of proof could well lead to a violation of a fundamental rule of procedure. It all depends on the importance, for the decision of the Tribunal, of the subject regarding which the burden has been reversed.").

135 RIDDELL & PLANT, *supra* note 17, at 123; Riddell, *supra* note 67, at 860.

136 Riddell, *supra* note 67, at 860.

137 *Id.*

138 ICJ Statute, Art. 53; *see also* EDUARDO VALENCIA-OSPINA, EVIDENCE BEFORE THE INTERNATIONAL COURT OF JUSTICE 203–204 (Int'l Law Forum du Droit Int'l 1999);

decision.[139] This part aims to piece together jurisprudence from the PCIJ, ICJ, and investor-state arbitration tribunals for clarification on standard of proof principles.

1 *Principle #1: Unlike Burden of Proof, Standard of Proof Is a Relative Concept*

Standard of proof is quite relative depending on the context of a particular issue before the tribunal. As early as the *Corfu Channel* case, the PCIJ/ICJ noted that standard of proof is variable; the determination of which standard of proof to apply is dependent on the matter in issue.[140] Judges after *Corfu Channel* have also reiterated this understanding.[141] Variable and unpredictable circumstances also sway the degree of standard of proof required in each case and within each case as well.[142] Factors including applicable substantive law, legal norms in question, and a tribunal's understanding of the context all contribute to the standard that is applicable for each relevant legal fact.[143] Sufficient evidence for one case may not end up being sufficient in another because of the relative nature of standard of proof.[144] Some commentators have been highly critical

139 AMERASINGHE, *supra* note 1, at 232–33; KAZAZI, *supra* note 17, at 325. *See also Tokios Tokelės v Ukraine*, ICSID Case No ARB/02/18, Award ¶ 124 (July 26, 2007) ("[w]e shall not propose a solution for the current uncertainty about the standard of proof to be applied in a case such as the present."); *Continental Casualty*, ICSID Case No ARB/03/9, at ¶ 135 ("The Committee notes that the ICSID Convention and the Arbitration Rules contain no provisions with respect to the burden of proof or standard of proof. Accordingly, there cannot be any requirement that a tribunal expressly apply a particular burden of proof or standard of proof in determining the dispute before it. Indeed, the tribunal is not obliged expressly to articulate any specific burden of proof or standard of proof and to analyse the evidence in those terms, as opposed simply to making findings of fact on the basis of the evidence before it.").

140 *Corfu Channel*, at 16–17.

141 *See Maritime Delimitation and Territorial Questions between Qatar and Bahrain*, Jurisdiction and Admissibility, Judgment, ICJ Reports 1995, at 63 (Feb. 15, 1995) (Dissenting Opinion of Judge Shahabuddeen) ("generally speaking, the standard of proof varies with the character of the particular issue of fact").

142 *Genocide Convention*, 77 ¶ 209–210 (requiring "proof at a high level of certainty appropriate to the seriousness of the allegation").

143 ROBERT KOLB, THE INTERNATIONAL COURT OF JUSTICE 944 (Hart Publishing 2013).

144 Allan Philip, Description in the Award of the Standard of Proof Sought and Satisfied, *in* Alan Redfern et al., The Standards and Burden of Proof in International Arbitration, 10 ARBITRATION INT'L 317, 361 (Kluwer Law Int'l 1994).

of tribunals that avoid a discussion clarifying the standard of proof, calling it an unjustifiable course of action given its importance in deciding a case.[145]

For those tribunals that have discussed standard of proof in the public international law context, it appears that there are generally three standards that a court may use in a non-criminal case: *prima facie*, balance of probabilities, and a heightened standard. The ICJ jurisprudence illustrate that all three types of standards can be applied in a hearing, depending on both the facts and the circumstances regarding the evidence.

1.1 Development of Case Law in PCIJ/ICJ

The Court has identified the relative nature of the standard of proof. When assessing evidence, the Court looks to the party with relatively stronger evidence.[146] Across many ICJ decisions, the Court assesses evidence in a manner that is dependent on the type of evidence they receive, and the context surrounding the case and the evidence itself. Some critics have deemed this manner of assessment to be incoherent and arbitrary.[147] However, the Court has more clearly articulated the requirements for meeting the standard of proof through discussion in several cases, including the *Nicaragua* case.

In *Nicaragua*, the Court explained how it evaluated particular types of evidence, including documentary evidence like press and broadcast materials, statements by State representatives, affidavits, government publications, and

145 *See, e.g.*, KAZAZI, *supra* note 17, at 325 ("[T]he fact that the standard of proof is usually not discussed by international tribunals is not justifiable. Even ongoing arbitral institutions which have adjudicated numerous international claims have normally refrained from providing a comprehensive discussion in this regard, or from explaining the underlying standard they have applied in their decisions."); AMERASINGHE, *supra* note 1, at 232–33 ("It would seem that both the ICJ and other international tribunals, including arbitral tribunals, which have adjudicated numerous international claims have usually not discussed in detail the matter of the standard of proof to be applied to the evaluated evidence and have not clearly explained the underlying standard they have applied in their decisions. On account of this a judge of the Iran-US Claims Tribunal was prompted to remark: 'It is regrettable that the Tribunal has never discussed the standard of proof it imposes on parties.' In some cases, however, international tribunals have addressed this question, in order to provide a general guideline for the evidentiary requirements in the cases being decided by them.").

146 *See Land, Island and Maritime Frontier Dispute; Sovereignty over Pulau Ligitan and Pulau Sipadan* (Indonesia v Malaysia), Judgment, Merits, [2002] ICJ Reports 625, 682 (Dec. 17, 2002).

147 *See, e.g., Democratic Republic of Congo v Uganda* (Dissenting Opinion of Judge ad hoc Kateka); *Nicaragua* (Dissenting Opinion of Judge Schwebel).

United Nations documents.[148] The court emphasized how different types of evidence were to be weighed differently in particular situations, and clarified that context contributes to the determination surrounding standard of proof.[149]

For example, statements that are against a party's interests are weighed according to the who the declarant of the statement is and the content of the statement itself.[150] As such, if the declarant of the statement is a high-ranking officer or representative of a State party, and the statement against interest was made in the declarant's official capacity, then the weight of this statement as evidence is substantial. These types of statements, if proven to actually be made by the declarant, carry an exceptional weight.[151] At the same time, there must be sufficient evidence that statements against interest are actually made for the court to give these statements credence.[152] As an example, statements broadcasted to the public, available in press before a litigation arose, or statements made during the course of prior litigation may serve as sufficient indicators that the statement was actually made by a declarant.

More generally speaking, the ICJ has described their approach in assessing evidence, and thereby, the standard of proof required, through their statement in *Democratic Republic of Congo v Uganda*. There, the court discussed the following:

> As it has done in the past, the Court will examine the facts relevant to each of the component elements of the claims advanced by the Parties. In so doing, it will identify the documents relied on and make its own clear assessment of their weight, reliability and value. In accordance with its prior practice, the Court will explain what items it should eliminate from further consideration.[153]

---

148 RIDDELL & PLANT, *supra* note 17, at 187.

149 *Id.*

150 *Nicaragua v United States*, Merits, Judgment, ICJ Reports 1986, at ¶ 64 (1986) (statements made by high-ranking state officials and political figures "are of particular probative value when they acknowledge facts or conduct unfavourable to the State represented by the person who made them", and can even be "construed as a form of admission").

151 RIDDELL & PLANT, *supra* note 17, at 188.

152 *Nicaragua v United States*, Merits, Judgment, ICJ Reports 1986, at ¶ 160 (courts should use caution and look to "the manner in which [these statements] were made public").

153 *Democratic Republic of Congo v Uganda*, at 59.

Categories of factors have also been laid out by ICJ jurisprudence in determining what evidence surpasses the standard of proof required for a party's success on a matter. These factors include:[154]

TABLE 3 Considerations in weighing evidence

Category	Consideration
Sources[155]	– The number of sources coming forth with the same evidence – Who the source is of the evidence? – Who submitted the evidence to the ongoing proceedings? – Whether the sources are impartial to the proceedings?
Degrees of Separation[156]	– Whether the evidence is observed, heard, or recorded first hand or not?

154 *See* RIDDELL & PLANT, *supra* note 17, at 192.

155 *See, e.g.*, Robert Pietrowski, Evidence in International Arbitration, 22 ARB. INT'L 373, 396 (2006) ("A witness' objectivity is often inferred from his relationship to the party on whose behalf he is testifying"); *Nicaragua*, at ¶ 70 ("A member of the government of a State engaged, not merely in international litigation, but in litigation relating to armed conflict, will probably tend to identify himself with the interests of his country, and to be anxious when giving evidence to say nothing which could prove adverse to its cause. The Court thus considers that it can certainly retain such parts of the evidence given by Ministers, orally or in writing, as may be regarded as contrary to the interests or contentions of the State to which the witness owes allegiance, or as relating to matters not controverted. For the rest, while in no way impugning the honour or veracity of the Ministers of either Party who have given evidence, the Court considers that the special circumstances of this case require it to treat such evidence with great reserve."); *Claims for Losses suffered in Belgium*, 2 UNRIAA 1011, 1040 (1930) (Transl.) ("In their appraisal of the evidence, the arbitrators will be obliged to be strict with regard to the prejudicial act, its author, and its date; for these are the very conditions of their competency.").

156 *See Corfu Channel*, at 17 ("The statements attributed by the witness Kovacic to third parties, of which the Court has received no personal and direct confirmation, can be regarded only as allegations falling short of conclusive evidence."); *Nicaragua*, at 42 ("Nor is testimony of matters not within the direct knowledge of the witness, but known to him only from hearsay, of much weight."). *See Corfu Channel*, at 17 ("The statements attributed by the witness Kovacic to third parties, of which the Court has received no personal and direct confirmation, can be regarded only as allegations falling short of conclusive evidence."); *Nicaragua*, at 42 ("Nor is testimony of matters not within the direct knowledge of the witness, but known to him only from hearsay, of much weight.").

TABLE 3 Considerations in weighing evidence (*cont.*)

Category	Consideration
Methodology	– How the evidence was collected or discovered?
	– Whether the evidence is written or orally repeated?[157]
	– Whether the evidence is based on expert analysis?[158]
Verification	– Whether there are means of verifying the information through corroboration or independent data?
	– Whether the evidence has subject to cross-examination?[159]
	– Whether the evidence reflects events that occurred under oath or was made under oath?
Timing	– At what point in time the evidence was prepared, collected, or made?[160]
	– Whether the evidence was created specifically for litigation?
Importance[161]	– How important and serious is the issue in question?[162]
	– Whether the issue is a highly-disputed one or not?
Procedure	– Whether the evidence properly followed procedural requirements when a party or third party submitted the evidence?

157 *See Nicaragua*, at 155 (Separate Opinion of President Nagendra Singh) ("the Court has not lost sight of the basic values in assessing the testimony and has noted the probative importance of [the] witness"); *Preah Vihear*, at 73 (Dissenting Opinion of Judge Moreno Quintana) ("the opinions of the experts and witnesses from Thailand impressed by their technical precision and the logical nature of their reasoning"); *Preah Vihear*, at 60 (Separate Opinion of Sir Gerald Fitzmaurice) ("could not help being struck by the evidence of one of Thailand's own expert witnesses-a patently honest and reliable one, it seemed to me").

158 *Preah Vihear*, at 58–59 (Separate Opinion of Judge Fitzmaurice) (cautioning the risk of relying too heavily on expert evidence); *Tunisia/Libya Continental Shelf*, Judgment, ICJ Reports 1982, at ¶ 41 (examining conflicting expert opinions).

159 See *Nicaragua*, at 42 ("the absence of the United States meant that the evidence of the witnesses presented by the Applicant at the hearings was not tested by cross-examination; however., those witnesses were subjected to extensive questioning from the bench"). *See also* RIDDELL & PLANT, *supra* note 17, at 194.

160 Courts have recognized the difficulty of procuring written evidence for events that occurred far in the past, and are more lenient in some special circumstances—even going as far as to lowering the standard of proof to "credible facts". *See* LI Sánchez Rodriguez, L'uti possidetis et les effectivités dans les contentieux territoriaux et frontaliers, 263 CCHAIL 295 (1997).

161 *Corfu Channel*, Merits, at 17 (noting that charges with less gravity can be substantiated with less evidence).

162 The ICJ courts have been seen to apply more relaxed standards of proof in cases regarding boundary disputes relative to cases that impugn State responsibilities or criminal activity. *See* Kolb, *supra* note 143, at 945.

Despite the availability of factors that ICJ jurisprudence has shown matter in making decisions regarding standard of proof, the ICJ has never formalized rules regarding assessment of evidence. It is true that the process of weighing evidence is not absolutely clear, but it is necessary for the standard of proof must be more relative than the burden of proof so that Courts are able to examine the evidence accordingly and freely.[163] A significant ability of the Court is to retain some amount of discretion in how evidence is analyzed. However, evaluating evidence can be too amorphous and arbitrary if courts do not explain their reasoning for how they have weighed the evidence; commentators have praised the efforts of Courts more recently in expressly examining the standard of proof, and the weight of evidence as well.[164]

1.2 Investor-State Tribunal Application

Investor-state tribunals have also noted that while burden of proof is absolute, standard of proof in investor-state arbitration is relative and will depend on the particular issue before the tribunal. The *Rompetrol v Romania* tribunal, for example, noted:

> [T]he Tribunal thinks that a word of clarification is in order, specifically as to the burden of proof vs. the standard of proof. The Tribunal believes that the distinction between the two can be stated quite simply: the burden of proof defines which party has to prove what, in order for its case to prevail; the standard of proof defines how much evidence is needed to establish either an individual issue or the party's case as a whole. As soon as the distinction is stated in that way, it becomes evident that the burden of proof is absolute, whereas the standard of proof is relative.[165]

Other investor-state tribunals have applied the same factors as listed in Table 4 in determining how to weigh evidence:

163 The principle of *freie Beweiswürdigung* (the free assessment of evidence) is crucial to a Court's task in resolving a dispute. *See Nicaragua*, at 40; *Case concerning certain German interests in Polish Upper Silesia (The merits)*, Judgment No. 7 (May 25, 1926) ("The Court is entirely free to estimate the value of statements made by the Parties.").

164 RIDDELL & PLANT, *supra* note 17, at 190.

165 *The Rompetrol Group NV v Romania*, ICSID Case No ARB/06/3, 178 (2013).

TABLE 4 Investor-state tribunal applications of factors

Category	Application
Sources	In *Generation Ukraine v Ukraine*, doubts regarding the credibility and reliability of evidence resulted in Claimant's failure to substantiate its allegations.[166]
Degrees of Separation	In *Moin v Iran*, the evidence was not heard firsthand and was reiterated as hearsay instead. The tribunal clarified that it could not rely on hearsay evidence unless it was substantiated.[167]
Methodology	In *SPP v Egypt*, the Tribunal found no need for expert opinions on disputed expenses when production of more information would suffice.[168]
Verification	In *Vacuum Salt v Ghana*, the tribunal accepted Claimant's request for oral proceedings due to the desirability of observing the witness and thereby giving a chance for live cross-examination.[169] Multiple investor-state tribunals have disregarded witness testimony when testimony was refuted as erroneous, untruthful,[170] or self-serving and inconsistent with the record.[171]

166 *Generation Ukraine v Ukraine*, ICSID, Award ¶¶ 19.2 *et seq.*, 19.15, 19.26 (Sept. 16, 2003) (boxes of documented source testimony were mistakenly thrown away and unable to be retrieved). *See also Rexnord Inc. v The Islamic Republic of Iran, et al.*, 2 Iran-U.S. CTR 6, 12 (Jan. 10, 1983).

167 *Jalal Moin v The Islamic Republic of Iran*, Case No 950, Award No 557-950-2, at ¶ 19 (May 24, 1994).

168 *Southern Pacific Properties ("SPP") (Middle East) Limited v Arab Republic of Egypt*, ICSID Case No ARB/84/3, Award ¶ 37 (May 20, 1992).

169 *Vacuum Salt Products Ltd. v Republic of Ghana*, ICSID Case No ARB/92/1, Award ¶ 45 (Feb. 16, 1994). *See also Tradex Hellas S.A. v Republic of Albania*, ICSID Case No ARB/94/2, Award ¶¶ 25–26, 34 (April 29, 1999) (allowing all witnesses to testify, claiming that credibility issues could be explored on cross-examination, and evaluating evidence based on consideration of these factors); *Santa Elena S.A. v Republic of Costa Rica*, ICSID Case No ARB/96/1, Award ¶ 49 (Feb. 17, 2000).

170 *See, e.g., Generation Ukraine v Ukraine*, ICSID Case No ARB/00/9, Award ¶ 19.7 (Sept. 16, 2003); *PSEG v Turkey*, ICSID, Award ¶¶ 177–178 (Jan. 19, 2007); *Fraport AG v Republic of Philippines*, ICSID Case No ARB/03/25, Award ¶¶ 328–329 (Aug. 16, 2007); *Vivendi v Argentina*, ICSID Case No ARB/97/3, Resubmitted Case: Award ¶¶ 4.13.7–4.13.10 (Aug. 20, 2007).

171 *Azinian v Mexico (AF)*, ICSID, Award ¶¶ 119, 122–123 (Nov. 1, 1999) (rejecting witness' statement as "self-serving" as well as inconsistent with the evidence record); *Plama v Bulgaria*,

TABLE 4 Investor-state tribunal applications of factors (*cont.*)

Category	Application
Importance	The IBA Rules on Evidence specifically allows tribunals to exclude evidence or not consider evidence that lacks "sufficient relevance … or materiality".[172]

Investor-state tribunals have not been required to explain all conflicting pieces of evidence when rendering their decision.[173] There are cases where the ICJ has expressed its decision when faced with conflicting evidence. The *El Salvador/Honduras* decision noted conflicting evidence given by opposing witnesses, but determined that "all in all, the Chamber does not consider much weight can be attached to this sparse testimony."[174] In the *Continental Shelf* case, the ICJ avoided the conflicting expert opinions by relying on a legal principle instead:

> The Court is unable to accept the position that in order to decide this case, it must first make a determination upon a disagreement between scientists of distinction as to the more plausibly correct interpretation of apparently incomplete scientific data; for a criterion that depends upon such a judgment or estimate having to be made by a court, or perhaps also by negotiating governments, is clearly inapt to a general legal rule of

Decision on Jurisdiction ¶¶ 177–178 (Feb. 8, 2005) (finding testimony to be unsupported by and materially inconsistent with the record); *Noble Ventures v Romania*, ICSID Case No ARB/01/11, Award ¶¶ 96–98 (Oct. 12, 2005) (refusing to rely on "uncorroborated and disputed evidence" from a witness); *Soufraki v United Arab Emirates*, ICSID Case No ARB/02/7, Award ¶¶ 78, 80–81 (July 7, 2004) (not finding witness affidavits to be "disinterested and convincing evidence" due to a financial relationship with Claimant).

172 IBA Rules on the Taking of Evidence in International Arbitration, Art. 9(2) (May 29, 2010) ("IBA Rules on Evidence").

173 *See CDC v Seychelles*, ICSID Case No ARB/02/14, Decision on Annulment ¶¶ 77, 83, 85 (June 29, 2005) (holding that not explaining conflicting witness statements did not mean that the Tribunal ignored evidence, but rather that the Tribunal came to a conclusion regarding the evidence with which the Applicant disagreed with); *MTD v Chile*, ICSID Case No ARB/01/7, Decision on Annulment ¶¶ 56–57 (March 21, 2007) (noting that Tribunal did not commit any procedural failure when it did not consider expert evidence that was presented by both Parties).

174 *Land, Island and Maritime Frontier Dispute* (*El Salvador/Honduras: Nicaragua intervening*), ICJ Judgment, at ¶ 276.

> delimitation. For all of the above reasons, the Court therefore rejects the so-called rift-zone argument of Libya.[175]

In offering a solution to this issue, commentators have encouraged parties to submit adequate evidence to ensure a "viable and fair resolution" of conflicting claims.[176]

2 *Principle #2: The Balance of Probabilities Standard or Preponderance of Evidence Standard*

2.1 Development of Case Law in PCIJ/ICJ

While neither the PCIJ nor the ICJ describes the different levels of standard of proof clearly, there is an overall sense of at least two basic standards of proof in international arbitrations. Commentators have described these as a general standard and an elevated standard.[177] The elevated standard will be discussed in Principle #3 in the following section. The general standard is also known as the most common standard of proof. It goes by various names, including balance of probabilities, preponderance of the evidence, or reasonable degree of probability.[178]

The general standard is understood to require the evidence to show that something is more likely than not. This understanding is parallel with the preponderance of the evidence standard.[179]

This general standard is also the most commonly used by the ICJ court. Though rarely discussed at length, the ICJ has shown that it uses the balance of probabilities to make decisions. For example, the court explains its use of balance of probabilities in the *Costa Rica v Nicaragua* case:

> The Court observes that there is no evidence that sediment due to the construction of the road is *more likely* to settle on the riverbed than sediment from other sources. Thus, sediment coming from the road would correspond to at most 2 per cent of the sediment dredged by Nicaragua in

175 *Tunisia/Libya Continental Shelf*, Judgment, ICJ Reports 1982, at ¶ 41.

176 MANI, *supra* note 23, at 198–199.

177 George M. von Mehren & Claudia T. Salomon, *Submitting Evidence in an International Arbitration: The Common Lawyer's Guide*, 20(3) J. INT'L ARBITRATION 291 (2003).

178 Pfitzer & Sabune, *supra* note 13 at 23; *Marion Unglaube and Reinhard Unglaube v Republic of Costa Rica*, ICSID Case Nos ARB/08/1 and ARB/09/20, Award 34 (May 16, 2012).

179 M. AGHAHOSSEINI, *Evidence Before the Iran-United States Claims Tribunal*, 1 INT'L LAW FORUM DU DROIT INT'L 208, 213 (1999) ("As is the case with the UNCITRAL Rules, the Tribunal Rules are silent with respect to the required standard of proof. In purely civil matters, the Tribunal has consistently imposed, as it should have, the standard of proof *on the preponderance of evidence*, alternatively described as *on the balance of probability*.").

> the Lower San Juan. The Court is *therefore not convinced* that the road-derived sediment led to a significant increase in the bed level of the Lower San Juan or in Nicaragua's dredging burden. (emphasis added)[180]

A few other tribunals have also used the "more likely", "more likely than not", or "on balance" terminology to describe their standard of proof analysis.[181]

2.2 Investor-State Tribunal Application

Investment tribunals summarize standard of proof as a balance of probabilities as well.[182] For example, the tribunal in *Kardassopoulos v Georgia* stated, "The Tribunal finds that the principle articulated by the vast majority of arbitral tribunals in respect of the burden of proof in international arbitration proceedings applies in these concurrent proceedings and does not impose on the Parties any burden of proof beyond balance of probabilities."[183] When tribunals make this application, they are generally weighing whether the evidence shows that the claim is more likely true than not true.[184] Civil lawyers use the

180 *Certain Activities Carried Out by Nicaragua in the Border Area (Costa Rica v Nicaragua) and Construction of a Road in Costa Rica along the San Juan River (Nicaragua v Costa Rica)*, Judgment, ICJ Reports 2015 ¶ 205 (Dec. 16, 2015).

181 *See, e.g., Sovereignty over Pedra Branca/Pulau Batu Puteh, Middle Rocks and South Ledge (Malaysia/Singapore)*, Judgment, ICJ Reports 2008 ¶ 133 (May 23, 2008) ("The Court is in no doubt that the proposal which the Governor put to the Government of India related to Peak Rock. Without knowing the contents of the Governor's earlier letters to the Sultan and Temenggong, the Court is however left in real doubt about what the Governor proposed. Judging from the two replies, *it would appear more likely than not* that his letters were in general terms. While Peak Rock was clearly the site he and his advisers had in mind, the final site of the lighthouse had yet to be decided upon.") (emphasis added); *Land, Island and Maritime Frontier Dispute (El Salvador/Honduras: Nicaragua intervening)*, Judgment, ICJ Reports 1992 ¶¶ 157, 200 (Sept. 11, 1992) ("Of the other two explanations put forward, the Chamber considers that advanced by Honduras, on balance, more likely."); *Territorial and Maritime Dispute between Nicaragua and Honduras in the Caribbean Sea (Nicaragua v Honduras)*, Judgment, ICJ Reports 2007 ¶ 161 (Oct. 8, 2007) ("On balance, the evidence presented in this case would seem to suggest that the Captaincy-General of Guatemala probably exercised jurisdiction over the areas north and south of Cape Gracias a Dios ..."); *Application for Review of Judgment No. 333 of the United Nations Administrative Tribunal*, Advisory Opinion, ICJ Reports 1987 ¶ 89 (May 27, 1987) (using "on balance" terminology).

182 *Marion Unglaube*, ICSID Case Nos ARB/08/1 and ARB/09/20, at 34.

183 *Ioannis Kardassopoulos and Ron Fuchs v Republic of Georgia*, ICSID Case Nos ARB/05/18 and ARB/07/15, Award ¶ 229 (March 3, 2010). *See also Bernhard von Pezold and Others v Republic of Zimbabwe*, ICSID Case No ARB/10/15, Award ¶ 177 (July 28, 2015) ("In general, the standard of proof applied in international arbitration is that a claim must be proven on the 'balance of probabilities.'").

184 O'MALLEY, *supra* note 28, at 208.

"inner conviction" test where the arbitrator must be personally satisfied with the evidence in order to resolve any issue. Commentators have noted that despite the difference in terminologies, there is no difference in the application of either formulation:

> None of the above-mentioned rules for international arbitration fix a standard of proof, however. The required standard of proof is often expressed by international arbitrators in terms of the jurisdiction from which they come. Whereas civil lawyers generally use the concept of the *intime conviction* of the arbitrator, common law lawyers talk in terms of a 'preponderance of the evidence' or 'a balance of probability'. However, 'in practice, the result is the same'.[185]

Some tribunals have expressly used the balance of probabilities and *intime* conviction test in the same breath when articulating the standard of proof. For example, the *Churchill v Indonesia* tribunal stated: "the Tribunal considers that the Respondent carries the burden of proving forgery and fraud, which proof will be measured on a standard of balance of probabilities or intime conviction taking into account that more persuasive evidence is required for implausible facts …"[186] Here, even though the tribunal paid lip-service to the balance of probabilities, it is in essence seeking a heightened standard for allegation of forgery.

The circumstances where balance of probabilities has been utilized in international arbitration include breach of contract claims, contractual clause interpretation, and investor-state claims arising from a breach of an international treaty.[187] It is usually the default rule. There are, however, limited circumstances where more heightened standards are utilized, as explained below in Principle 3.

Another area where investor-state tribunals have generally applied the balance of probabilities standard is during the damages calculation phase of an arbitration. The *Crystallex v Venezuela* tribunal goes through an analysis of the standard of proof used during the damages phase, which elucidates the reason for the use of balance of probabilities. First, as balance of probabilities is

---

185 Vera Van Houtte, *Adverse Inferences in International Arbitration* in Teresa Giovannini and Alexis Mouree (eds), WRITTEN EVIDENCE AND DISCOVERY IN INTERNATIONAL ARBITRATION: NEW ISSUES AND TENDENCIES 198 (Dossiers ICC Institute of World Business Law 2009). *L'intime conviction* translates to inner conviction.

186 *Churchill Mining and Planet Mining Pty Ltd v Republic of Indonesia*, ICSID Case Nos ARB/12/14 and 12/40, Award ¶ 244 (Dec. 6, 2016).

187 O'MALLEY, *supra* note 28, at 208.

the same standard used in the liability and merits portion of the case, there is no reason why the standard would not also apply to damages.[188] Essentially, since the tribunal must believe with the same conviction that damages exists, the standard should be the same. Second, a standard lower than balance of probabilities is expected when calculating for future damages, as it is inherently an estimate of what can happen.[189]

3 *Principle #3: The Heightened Standard of Proof*

3.1 Development of Case Law in PCIJ/ICJ

More recent ICJ cases have distinguished a standard that is higher than a preponderance of the evidence standard concerning claims surrounding graver issues, such as genocide and corruption.[190] In the *Judgment for the Application of Genocide Convention between Croatia and Serbia*, the tribunal defines the standard of proof used as "[e]vidence must be 'fully conclusive'—[a] [c]ourt must be 'fully convinced' that acts have been committed."[191]

Development of case law in the ICJ regarding claims against States has been fairly consistent in applying a higher standard of proof for cases made against States, especially cases in which States have been accused of "charges of exception[al] gravity".[192] From the 1949 *Corfu Channels* case, which required "decisive legal proof" in order to find "conclusive evidence", to the 2007 *Bosnia* case, which stated that "claims against a State involving charges of exceptional

188 *Crystallex International Corp v Bolivarian Republic of Venezuela*, ICSID Case No ARB(AF)/11/2, Award ¶¶ 867–69, 871 (April 4, 2016).

189 *Id.; see also Joseph Charles Lemire v Ukraine*, ICSID Case No ARB/06/18, Award (March 28, 2011), ¶¶ 246–247 ("Once causation has been established, and it has been proven that the in bonis party has indeed suffered a loss, less certainty is required in proof of the actual amount of damages; for this latter determination Claimant only needs to provide a basis upon which the Tribunal can, with reasonable confidence, estimate the extent of the loss.").

190 Alan Redfern, Claude Reymond, Andreas Reiner, Bernard Hanotiau, Edward Lord Eveleigh, Ian W Menzies, and Allan Philip, *The Standards and Burden of Proof in International Arbitration*, 10(5) Arbitration Int'l 335 (1994) ("Both, the Anglo-Saxon and the continental systems require higher standards of proof for particularly important or delicate questions such as bribery or other types of fraud."); *Waguih Elie George Siag v Arab Republic of Egypt*, ICSID Case No ARB/05/15, Award ¶ 326 (June 1, 2009) ("It is common in most legal systems for serious allegations such as fraud to be held to a high standard of proof.").

191 *Application of the Convention on the Prevention and Punishment of the Crime of Genocide (Croatia v Serbia)*, Judgment, ICJ Reports 2015, at 10 (2015).

192 *Pulp Mills on the River Uruguay (Argentina v Uruguay)*, Judgment, ICJ Reports 2010, Merits, Separate Opinion of Judge Greenwood ¶ 25 (2010).

gravity must be proved by evidence that is *fully conclusive*." (emphasis added)[193] In understanding the factors that weigh towards or against a heightened standard of proof, the courts look to how serious the allegations are and then subsequently analyze the evidence in the following manner, as suggested in the *Bosnia* case:

> [D]epends, among other things, on (1) the source of the item of evidence (for instance partisan, or neutral), (2) the process by which it has been generated (for instance an anonymous press report or the product of a careful court or court-like process), and (3) the quality or character of the item (such as statements against interest, and agreed or uncontested facts).[194]

These echo the factors that are considered in determining the standard of proof needed as well, as set forth in Table 3 above. Even though the court acknowledged a heightened standard of proof in the circumstances presented in *Bosnia*, it is crucial to note that the Court rejected the Respondent's even stricter standard that was closer to a beyond reasonable doubts standard reserved usually for criminal cases.[195] Commentators have noted that the beyond reasonable doubts standard does not belong in non-criminal cases.[196]

3.2 Investor-State Tribunal Application

Heightened standard of proof may apply in more specific circumstances in investor-state disputes as well.

---

193 *Corfu Channel*, Merits, Judgment, ICJ Reports 1949, at 17 (April 9, 1949); *Genocide Convention (Bosnia)*, Merits, Judgment, ICJ Reports 2007 ¶ 209 (Feb. 26, 2007). *See also Qatar v Bahrain Jurisdiction and Admissibility II*, Dissenting Opinion of Judge Shahabuddeen, ICJ Reports 1995, at 63 (1995); *Land, Island and Maritime Frontier Dispute (El Salvador/Honduras), Application to Zntewene*, Judgment, ICJ Reports 1990 ¶ 61 (September 13, 1990) (requiring party to "demonstrate convincingly what it asserts"); *Oil Platforms (Islamic Republic of Iran v United States of America)*, Judgment, ICJ Reports 2003 ¶ 71 (Nov. 6, 2003) (failing to find for a party when their "evidence is highly suggestive, but not conclusive").

194 Bosnia, ICJ Reports 2007 (I), at ¶ 227; *see also United States Diplomatic and Consular Staff in Tehran*, Judgment, ICJ Reports 1980, ¶ 11–13 (1980); *Military and Paramilitary Activities in and against Nicaragua (Nicaragua v United States of America)*, Merits, Judgment, ICJ Reports 1986, at ¶ 59–73; *Armed Activities on the Territory of the Congo (Democratic Republic of the Congo v Uganda)*, Judgment, ICJ Reports 2005, at ¶ 57–61.

195 *Armed Activities on the Territory of the Congo*, at ¶ 208.

196 AGHAHOSSEINI, *supra* note 179, at 213; JUAN JOSÉ QUINTANA, LITIGATION AT THE INTERNATIONAL COURT OF JUSTICE: PRACTICE AND PROCEDURE 407 (Brill 2015).

3.2.1 *Requirements Expressly Provided for in the Rules*

First, a few investment tribunals include procedural rules that require a heightened standard of proof. For example, Article 57 of the ICSID Convention sets the standard of proof at "manifest" lack of qualifications when challenging an arbitrator.[197] Similarly, ICSID Arbitration Rule 41(5) also sets the standard of proof at "manifestly without legal merit",[198] which has been interpreted by tribunals to mean a clear and obvious standard when dealing with an argument brought by a state to seek an early dismissal of the case.[199]

3.2.2 *Quasi-Criminal Allegations*

Second, when allegations of a quasi-criminal nature have surfaced, there is tension regarding standard of proof and this question remains unsettled. Several tribunals have used a heightened standard, citing the serious consequences that stem from these claims, if proven true.[200] The majority tribunal in *Siag v Egypt* stated: "It is common in most legal systems for serious allegations such as fraud to be held to a high standard of proof."[201] In fact, arbitrators following

197 ICSID Convention, Art. 57 ("A party may propose to a Commission or Tribunal the disqualification of any of its members on account of any fact indicating a manifest lack of the qualities required by paragraph (1) of Article 14.").

198 ICSID Arbitration Rules, Rule 41(5) ("Unless the parties have agreed to another expedited procedure for making preliminary objections, a party may, no later than 30 days after the constitution of the Tribunal, and in any event before the first session of the Tribunal, file an objection that a claim is manifestly without legal merit.").

199 *PNG Sustainable Development Program Ltd v Independent State of Papua New Guinea*, ICSID Case No ARB/13/33, The Tribunal's Decision on the Respondent's Objections Under Rule 41(5) of the ICSID Arbitration Rule 88, 91 (October 28, 2014); *Trans-Global Petroleum, Inc. v Hashemite Kingdom of Jordan*, ICSID Case No ARB/07/25, Decision on the Respondent's Objection under Rule 41(5) of the ICSID Arbitration Rules 86 (May 12, 2008).

200 *European Media Ventures SA v Czech Republic*, UNCITRAL, Partial Award on Liability 35 (July 8, 2009); *Liman Caspian Oil BV and NCL Dutch Investment BV v Republic of Kazakhstan*, ICSID Case No ARB/07/14, Excerpts of Award 422–424 (June 22, 2010). *But see Libananco Holdings Co Ltd v Republic of Turkey*, ICSID Case No ARB/06/8, Award ¶ 125 (Sept. 2, 2011) ("In relation to the Claimant's contention that there should be a heightened standard of proof for allegations of 'fraud or other serious wrongdoing', the Tribunal accepts that fraud is a serious allegation, but it does not consider that this (without more) requires it to apply a heightened standard of proof. While agreeing with the general proposition that 'the graver the charge, the more confidence there must be in the evidence relied on', this does not necessarily entail a higher standard of proof. It may simply require more persuasive evidence, in the case (p. 95) of a fact that is inherently improbable, in order for the Tribunal to be satisfied that the burden of proof has been discharged.").

201 *Waguih Elie George Siag v Arab Republic of Egypt*, ICSID Case No ARB/05/15, Award ¶ 326 (June 1, 2009). The dissenting arbitrator in the case disagreed with the standard of proof applied by the majority preferring instead to apply a discretionary standard of proof. *Waguih Elie George Siag v Arab Republic of Egypt*, ICSID Case No ARB/05/15, Dissenting

a heightened approach have contended that wrongdoing allegations ought to be disregarded entirely unless substantiated sufficiently.[202] Tribunals, however, have often been inconsistent about what a heightened standard of proof entails. Some tribunals describe the standard as akin to a "clear and convincing" standard, others simply note that the standard is "high" or "demanding" without further analysis,[203] or, as noted in *Churchill v Indonesia*, a tribunal may simply mean that "more persuasive evidence" is needed, without citing to a particular standard at all.[204] Indeed, the *Libananco Holdings* tribunal, noted that:

> In relation to the Claimant's contention that there should be a heightened standard of proof for allegations of 'fraud or other serious wrongdoing', the Tribunal accepts that fraud is a serious allegation, but it does not consider that this (without more) requires it to apply a heightened standard of proof. While agreeing with the general proposition that 'the graver the charge, the more confidence there must be in the evidence relied on', this does not necessarily entail a higher standard of proof. It may simply require more persuasive evidence, in the case … of a fact that

Opinion of Professor Francisco Orrego Vicuña ¶ 13 (June 1, 2009) (disagreeing with applicable standard of proof because arbitration tribunals "are free to choose the most relevant rules in accordance with the circumstances of the case and the nature of the facts involved"; the standard the Tribunal should use is "discretion in inferring from a collection of concordant circumstantial evidence (*faisceau d'indices*) the facts at which the various indices are directed.") (internal citations and quotations omitted).

202 *International Thunderbird Gaming Corp v United Mexican States*, UNCITRAL, Separate Opinion of Professor Wälde 20 (December 1, 2005) ("The same applies to the corruption hint insinuated by respondent in its submission … Such insinuations are now frequently employed by both claimant investors and respondent governments. They should be disregarded—explicitly submitted to the tribunal, substantiated with a specific allegation of corruption and subject to proper legal and factual debate for the tribunal."); *Himpurna California Energy Ltd v PT (Persero) Perusahaan Listruik Negara*, Final Award ¶ 114, 118 (May 4, 1999) ("[accusations] must be treated with great circumspection.… The arbitrators believe that cronyism and other forms of abuse of public trust do indeed exist in many countries.… But such grave accusations must be proven.").

203 *Bayindir Insaat Turizm Ticaret Ve Sanayi AS v Islamic Republic of Pakistan*, ICSID Case No ARB/03/29, Award (August 27, 2009), ¶ 143 ("The Tribunal further considers that, as argued by the Respondent, the standard for proving bad faith is a *demanding* one, in particular if bad faith is to be established on the basis of circumstantial evidence.") (emphasis added); *see also Chemtura Corporation (formerly Crompton Corporation) v Government of Canada*, UNCITRAL-NAFTA, Award 137 (August 2, 2010) (citing *Bayindir* with approval).

204 *Churchill Mining PLC and Planet Mining Pty Ltd v Republic of Indonesia*, ICSID Case Nos ARB/12/14 and 12/40, Award 244 (December 6, 2016).

is inherently improbable, in order for the Tribunal to be satisfied that the burden of proof has been discharged.[205]

Some tribunals have followed this particular approach.[206] A few tribunals have also reached a conclusion regarding corruption even through indirect or circumstantial evidence.[207] There are also a few special circumstances where tribunals have applied a heightened standard to issues involving some forms of corruption,[208] illegal investments,[209] and forgery.[210]

Some examples of how tribunals have discussed corruption allegations include the following: In *World Duty Free v Kenya*, the investor admitted he had made a "personal donation" of US$ 500,000 to a former president of Kenya and justified such payment on the fact that it was common under cultural

205 *Libananco Holdings Co Ltd v Republic of Turkey*, ICSID Case No ARB/06/8, Award ¶ 125 (Sept. 2, 2011).

206 *See Tokios Tokelés v Ukraine*, ICSID Case No. ARB/02/18, Award ¶ 124 (26 July 2007).

207 *See Metal-Tech v Republic of Uzbekistan*, ICSID Case No. ARB/10/3, Award (Oct. 4, 2013), ¶ 243 (the Tribunal would "determine on the basis of the evidence before it whether corruption has been established with reasonable certainty', noting in this context 'that corruption is by essence difficult to establish and that it is thus generally admitted that it can be shown through circumstantial evidence."); *Europe Cement v Turkey*, ICSID Case No. ARB(AF)/07/2 ¶ 167 (Aug. 13, 2009) ("the Tribunal has no direct evidence that any particular document placed before it was or was not authentic, but the implication of lack of authenticity is overwhelming.... Indeed, the evidence points to the conclusion that the claim to ownership of the shares at a time that would establish jurisdiction was made fraudulently").

208 *European Media Ventures*, at 35; *Liman Caspian Oil*, at 422–424; *EDF (Services) Ltd v Romania*, ICSID Case No ARB/05/13, Award ¶ 221 (October 8, 2009) ("There is general consensus among international tribunals and commentators regarding the need for a high standard of proof of corruption. The evidence before the Tribunal in the instant case concerning the alleged solicitation of a bribe is far from being clear and convincing.").

209 *Energoalians SARL v Republic of Moldova*, UNCITRAL, Award 261 (October 23, 2013).

210 *Dadras International and Per-Am Construction Corporation v Islamic Republic of Iran and Tehran Redevelopment Company*, Award No 567–213/215–3 ¶¶ 123–124 (1995); MOSK, *supra* note 104, at 137 ("The Iran-United States Claims Tribunal did state that because "allegations of forgery" are "particularly grave", to establish such an allegation requires "an enhanced standard of proof."") There are a few other examples of a heightened standard in particular instances. *See Anatolie Stati, Gabriel Stati, Ascom Group SA, and Terra Raf Trans Trading Ltd v Republic of Kazakhstan*, SCC Case No V116/2010, Award 1688 (December 19, 2013) ("[T]he investor must meet a high standard of proof to establish a claim for lost profits, especially due to the degree of economic, political, and social exposure of long-term investment projects.").

practices.[211] The tribunal rejected these arguments and concluded that the payment was a bribe.[212] In *Metal-Tech v Uzbekistan*, large sums of money had been paid to consultants and the question was whether these sums of money had been paid as a bribe or for lawful services.[213] The evidence ultimately produced was minimal and could not provide a satisfactory explanation for the large sums. This led the tribunal to ultimately conclude that the "Claimant was unable to substantiate its contention that actual services had been carried out for legitimate purposes."[214] The failure to present satisfactory evidence despite being provided an opportunity to do so led to the dismissal of the case.

Citing the serious nature of some wrongdoing allegations, a few commentators suggest that a criminal standard of proof-equivalent should apply in the most extreme of circumstances relating to corruption and bribery.[215] No investment arbitration tribunal has followed this methodology, though a few have vaguely described a heightened standard in the most extreme scenarios.[216]

IV Conclusion

This article seeks to understand the influence of ICJ jurisprudence on investor-state tribunals when it comes to issues relating to burden and standard of

211 *World Duty Free Co. Ltd. v Republic of Kenya*, ICSID Case No ARB/00/7, Award (Oct. 4, 2006), ¶¶ 66, 130.

212 *Id.*, ¶ 136.

213 *Metal-Tech v Republic of Uzbekistan*, ICSID Case No ARB/10/3, Award (Oct. 4, 2013), ¶¶ 244–266.

214 *Id.* The question before the tribunal was whether the term "implemented" meant "established" or "established and operated." *Id.*, ¶ 185. Undertaking an interpretative exercise, the tribunal concluded that "asset implemented" referred to the "time when the investment was made" and that "the investment must be legal when it is initially established." *Id.*, ¶ 193.

215 Richard Kreindler, 'Application for "Revision" in Investment Arbitration: Selected Current Issues' in M Á FERNÁNDEZ-BALLESTEROS & DAVID ARIAS, LIBER AMICORUM BERNARDO CREMADES 691 (Wolters Kluwer 2010) ("At the same time, precisely because of the seriousness of an alleged offense of corruption or bribery, it is likewise a well-established principle in public international law, as well as in civil law, that the standard of proof respecting allegations of corruption is elevated, and cannot be justified by mere speculation. Especially criminal allegations or quasi-criminal allegations of corruption demand a high standard of evidence; the existence of corruption must be proven beyond a reasonable doubt.").

216 *See, e.g.*, ICC Award No 8891, J. DROIT INT'L 1076 (2000) (finding that serious pieces of evidence must exist to establish bribery).

proof. There are two preliminary points that are in order: first, neither the Statute of the ICJ nor most international investment agreements do not provide any detailed guidance on matters relating to burden and standard of proof, and, second, both the ICJ and investor-state tribunals do not provide much meaningful guidance on these matters.

As a general matter, investor-state tribunals have followed the jurisprudence of the ICJ on matters relating to burden and standards of proof. For example, the *actori incumbit onus probandi* principle as recognized by the ICJ has been consistently applied by investor-state tribunals. Further, the *pro tem* rule famously developed by Judge Higgins is ubiquitously applied by investor-state tribunals for jurisdictional issues.

On matters of standard of proof, there is a difference between ICJ jurisprudence (which can deal with a wide-range of issues including civil and criminal matters) and the jurisprudence of investor-state tribunals (which deals with civil law breaches with limited quasi-criminal issues on wrongdoings). There is a tendency to follow the ICJ jurisprudence here where both bodies insist on additional, more persuasive evidence based on the nature of the allegation—namely, the more serious the allegation, the more demanding the standard of proof is. This is another area where investor-state tribunals follow the general jurisprudence as developed by tribunals and accordingly follows the factors for consideration in weighing evidence.

Considering the impact that the burden of and standards of proof have in any given case, it is hoped that both ICJ and investor-state tribunals clarify these issues more carefully in the future. As more tribunals continue to explain their rationale in allocating and analyzing evidence, the hope is that evidentiary principles will become further coherent, leading to more consistency in the adjudicative process.

As noted by John Adams: "*Facts are stubborn things; and whatever may be our wishes, our inclinations, or the dictates of our passions, they cannot alter the state of facts and evidence.*"

Acknowledgments

The authors express with gratitude the insights from Professors Eric de Brabandere, Director of the Grotius Centre at Leiden Law School and Dr. Mamadou Hébié at the International Court of Justice for creating an interest in this topic, Professor George Bermann and Professor Rob Smit at Columbia Law School for their support and encouragement, Professor Ian Laird and Professor Frédéric Sourgens for many discussions on evidentiary issues,

Ms. Giovanna Gismondi Luis at Georgetown Law School for reviewing the article, Ms. Johanna Lee at Brill for all her support, and Ms. Diora Ziyaeva for peer reviewing the article. The views expressed are personal and do not reflect the views of any of the institutions we are affiliated with. The authors reserve the right to supplement or change the opinion based on developments in the law. All errors remain our own.

Bibliography

Aghahosseini, Mohsen, Evidence Before the Iran-United States Claims Tribunal, 1 INT'L LAW FORUM DU DROIT INT'L 208 (1999).

Amerasinghe, Chittharanjan, Evidence in International Litigation (2005).

Amerasinghe, Chittharanjan, Law of the International Civil Service (1994).

Binder, Peter, Analytical Commentary to the UNCITRAL Arbitration Rules 262 (2013).

Buergenthal, Thomas, Judicial Fact-Finding: The Inter-American Human Rights Court, in Fact-Finding by International Tribunals (Lillich ed. 1991).

Cheng, Bin, General Principles of Law as applied by International Courts and Tribunals (2006).

Clermont, Kevin M. & Emily Sherwin, A Comparative View of Standards of Proof, 50 AM. J. COMP. L. 243 (2002).

Clermont, Kevin M., Procedure's Magical Number Three: Psychological Bases for Standards of Decision, 72 CORNELL L. REV. 1115 (1987).

Frowein, Jochen A., Fact-Finding by the European Commission on Human Rights, in Fact-Finding by International Tribunals (Lillich ed. 1991).

Glendon, Mary Ann, Michael Wallace Gordon & Christopher Osakwe, Comparative Legal Traditions (1985).

Grando, Michelle Terezinha, The Process of Fact-Finding before International Tribunals: A Study of the WTO Dispute Settlement System (2008).

Hanotiau, Bernard, Satisfying the Burden of Proof; The Viewpoint of a 'Civil Law' Lawyer, in Alan Redfern et al., The Standards and Burden of Proof in International Arbitration, 10 ARBITRATION INT'L 317 (Kluwer Law Int'l 1994).

Heydon, J.D., Cases and Materials on Evidence (Butterworths, London, 1975).

IBA Rules on the Taking of Evidence in International Arbitration (May 29, 2010).

Kaplan, Benjamin, Arthur T. von Mehren & Rudolf Schaefer, Phases of German Civil Procedure I, 71 HARV. L. REV. 1193 (1957).

Kazazi, Mojtaba, Burden of Proof and Related Studies: A Study on Evidence Before International Tribunals (Kluwer Law International 1995).

Kokott, Juliane, The Burden of Proof in Comparative and International Human Rights Law (1996).

Kolb, Robert, The International Court of Justice (Hart Publishing 2013).

Kreindler, Richard, Application for "Revision" in Investment Arbitration: Selected Current Issues, in M.Á. Fernández-Ballesteros & David Arias, Liber Amicorum Bernardo Cremades (Wolters Kluwer 2010).

Lew, Julian D.M., 'Document Disclosure, Evidentiary Value of Documents and Burden of Evidence' in Teresa Giovannini and Alexis Mouree (eds), Written Evidence and Discovery in International Arbitration: New Issues and Tendencies (Dossiers ICC Institute of World Business Law 2009).

Mani, V.S., International Adjudication: Procedural Aspects (1980).

Maritime Arbitration Association of the United States, Arbitration Rules, *available at* http://www.maritimearbitration.com/File-a-Case/Arbitration-Rules.

Martin, A.T., International Arbitration and Corruption: An Evolving Standard (2004), *available at* https://www.transnational-dispute-management.com/article.asp?key=88.

Mosk, Richard M., The Role of Facts in International Dispute Resolution (Recueil des cours 2003).

Nappert, Sophie, Commentary on the UNCITRAL Arbitration Rules 2010: A Practitioner's Guide 103–04 (2012).

O'Malley, Nathan D., Rules of Evidence in International Arbitration: An Annotated Guide (Informa 2012).

PCIJ, Twenty-Fifth Meeting, Continuation of the discussion on the Draft Rules of Court submitted by the Drafting Committee 142 (March 9, 1922), *available at* http://www.icj-cij.org/files/permanent-court-of-international-justice/serie_D/D_02_preparation_reglement.pdf.

Pfitzer, James H. & Sheila Sabune, Burden of Proof in WTO Dispute Settlement: Contemplating Preponderance of the Evidence, 9 ICTSD DISPUTE SETTLEMENT AND LEGAL ASPECTS OF INT'L TRADE 6 (April 2009).

Philip, Allan, Description in the Award of the Standard of Proof Sought and Satisfied, *in* Alan Redfern et al., The Standards and Burden of Proof in International Arbitration, 10 ARBITRATION INT'L 361 (Kluwer Law Int'l 1994).

Pietrowski, Robert, Evidence in International Arbitration, 22 ARB. INT'L 373 (2006).

Quintana, Juan José, Litigation at the International Court of Justice: Practice and Procedure (Brill 2015).

Redfern, Alan, Claude Reymond, Andreas Reiner, Bernard Hanotiau, Edward Lord Eveleigh, Ian W. Menzies, and Allan Philip, The Standards and Burden of Proof in International Arbitration, 10 ARBITRATION INT'L 335 (Kluwer Law Int'l 1994).

Reymond, Claude, The Practical Distinction Between the Burden of Proof and Taking of Evidence—A Further Perspective, 10 ARBITRATION INT'L 326 (1994).

Riddell, Anna & Brendan Plant, Evidence Before the International Court of Justice (2009).

Riddell, Anna, 'Evidence, Fact-Finding, and Experts' in Cesare P.R. Romano, Karen J. Alter and Yuval Shany (eds), The Oxford Handbook of International Adjudication (Oxford University Press 2014).

Sanchez Rodriguez, L.I., L'uti possidetis et les effectivités dans les contentieux territoriaux et frontaliers, 263 CCHAIL 295 (1997).

Sandifer, Durward V., Evidence Before International Tribunals 126–127 (1939).

Schreuer, Christoph H. et al., The ICSID Convention: A Commentary 669 (2009).

Statute of the International Court of Justice (ICJ), 14 April 1978 (Amended on 14 April 2005).

Statute of the Permanent Court of International Justice (PCIJ), 16 December 1920 (Amended by the Protocol of September 14, 1929), available at http://www.icj-cij.org/files/permanent-court-of-international-justice/serie_D/D_01_4e_edition.pdf.

Valencia-Ospina, Eduardo, Evidence before the International Court of Justice, 1 INT'L L. FORUM DU DROIT INT'L 202 (1999).

Van Houtte, Vera, 'Adverse Inferences in International Arbitration' in Teresa Giovannini and Alexis Mouree (eds), Written Evidence and Discovery in International Arbitration: New Issues and Tendencies (Dossiers ICC Institute of World Business Law 2009).

von Mehren, George M. & Claudia T. Salomon, Submitting Evidence in an International Arbitration: The Common Lawyer's Guide, 20 J. INT'L ARBITRATION 285 (2003).

Waincymer, Jeffrey, Procedure and Evidence in International Arbitration (2012).

World Trade Organization (WTO), Dispute Settlement Understanding (DSU) Annex 2, Understanding on Rules and Procedures Governing the Settlement Of Disputes, available at https://www.wto.org/english/Tratop_e/dispu_e/dsu_e.htm.

Zimmermann, Andreas et al., The Statute of the International Court of Justice: A Commentary (2d ed. 2012).

Other Titles in International Investment Law and Arbitration

Damages in Investor-State Arbitration: Current Issues and Challenges

Irmgard Marboe ISBN *9789004366855*

The assessment of damages in investor-state arbitration involves complex legal and economic considerations. Particular challenges arise from the interdisciplinary nature of this endeavor. The present issue discusses some of the pertinent specificities in investor-state disputes reflecting the tensions between sovereignty and self-determination of states and their legal obligations towards foreign investors. These tensions are primarily present in the context of expropriation, but also commitments undertaken by states in bilateral investment treaties and contracts as well as changing economic circumstances need to be taken into consideration. The lack of valuation principles that are uniformly accepted and implemented leads to uncertainty and unpredictability in practice. The present volume analyses some of the most controversial and unsettled issues, including the choice of the valuation date, appropriate valuation methods, moral damages, and the awarding of interest.

Jurisdiction and Admissibility in Investment Arbitration: The Practice and the Theory

Filippo Fontanelli *ISBN 9789004366480*

This is the first half of a two-part essay on jurisdiction and admissibility in investment arbitration. It focuses on the arbitration practice, whilst the second part sets these concepts in the wider framework of public international law litigation. This essay maps the objections to the tribunal's jurisdiction (by *ratio: materiae, temporis, loci* and *personae*) and the claim's admissibility. It offers some preliminary conclusions: in certain areas there still is no consensus; tribunals are inclined to characterise objections as jurisdictional, and rarely resort to admissibility; findings of inadmissibility draw a judgment on the claimant or the claim's propriety (whilst jurisdictional decisions typically eschew value-judgment); tribunals failed to distinguish jurisdiction from admissibility. These findings are further explored, within a wider theoretical context, in the second part of the essay.

Fair and Equitable Treatment: Its Interaction with the Minimum Standard and its Customary Status

Patrick Dumberry ISBN 9789004366114

The book addresses two questions which have been debated by scholars in the last 20 years regarding the fair and equitable treatment ('FET') standard found in BITs. It examines the interaction between the 'minimum standard of treatment' (MST) and the FET standard. It first analyses the fascinating story of how the concept of the MST emerged in the early 20th Century, its subsequent decline from 1960s until the 1990s and its surprising recent 'resurrection' in the year 2000. This evolution has had a direct impact on the emergence and subsequent development of the FET standard and explains why States started referring to that standard instead of the MST in their investment treaties. One question addressed in this book, is whether FET is an autonomous standard of protection to be accorded to foreign investors, or is a mere reference to the MST under customary international law. Given the fact that the FET standard is found in the overwhelming majority of BITs, another question which arose is whether or not it should now be considered in and of itself as a rule of customary international law.

International Investment Law and Arbitration: History, Modern Practice, and Future Prospects

Borzu Sabahi, Ian A. Laird and Giovanna E. Gismondi ISBN 9789004366480

International Investment Law is one of the most dynamically growing fields of International Law as shown by the volume of Bilateral Investment Treaties (BITS), and investment chapters in a growing numbers of regional and mega-regional trade agreements. This paper explores the origin, evolution and operation of International Investment Law. It discusses the main actors, the protections afforded to foreign investments and investors, and the content of modern BITS. The legal issues and challenges International Investment Law faces today are brought into perspective. Particularly, this paper provides an assessment of the measures put forth by the European Union aimed at transforming the traditional investor-State arbitration system to an Investment Court System. An examination of the NAFTA re-negotiations is also presented, including the impact that CETA, a trade deal between the EU and Canada could have in the outcome of the current re-negotiations.

Print Book Orders and Journal Subscription

Customers outside the Americas

BRILL
c/o Turpin Distribution
Stratton Business Park
Pegasus Drive
Biggleswade
Bedfordshire SG18 8TQ
United Kingdom
T +44 (0) 1767 604-954
F +44 (0) 1767 601-640
brill@turpin-distribution.com

Customers in the Americas

BRILL
c/o Turpin Distribution
143 West Street
New Milford, CT 06776
United States
T (844) 232 3707 (Toll free US and Canada)
T +1 (860) 350 0041
F +1 (860) 350 0039
brillna@turpin-distribution.com

Online Resources and Primary Sources

Customers outside the Americas

BRILL
P.O. Box 9000
2300 PA Leiden
The Netherlands
T +31 (0)71-53 53 500
F +31 (0)71-53 17 532
sales-nl@brill.com

Customers in the Americas

BRILL
2 Liberty Square, 11th Floor
Boston, MA 02109
United States
T 1-617-263-2323
F 1-617-263-2324
sales-us@brill.com

www.ingramcontent.com/pod-product-compliance
Lightning Source LLC
Chambersburg PA
CBHW071400230926
51846CB00002B/602